TRUSTING IN SPIRIT - THE CHALLENGE

DR. BOB WOODWARD

authorHOUSE®

AuthorHouse™ UK
1663 Liberty Drive
Bloomington, IN 47403 USA
www.authorhouse.co.uk
Phone: 0800.197.4150

Published by AuthorHouse 04/16/2018

ISBN: 978-1-5462-9162-6 (sc)
ISBN: 978-1-5462-9163-3 (hc)
ISBN: 978-1-5462-9161-9 (e)

Print information available on the last page.

CONTENTS

Also by Bob Woodward:
Spirit Healing (2004)
Spirit Communications (2007)
Spiritual Healing with Children with Special Needs (2007)

And with Dr Marga Hogenboom
Autism – A Holistic Approach (third edition 2013)

FOREWORD

I became acquainted with Bob Woodward in 2004 when he requested a spiritual reading from me. His guides started to introduce themselves, Joshua and Dr John. Since that time Bob has consistently dedicated his life to spiritual development by sitting in the silence. This has allowed his spiritual gifts to develop, allowing a deep relationship with his guides based on truth and understanding.

As an academic his logical approach and open enquiring mind encouraged huge development and this book is the unique culmination of their shared gifts, both physical and spiritual. This is Spirit's book for you the reader, whether a non-believer, new to the idea or experienced in spirit communication.

Spirit guides and teachers wish to share with you the tools to live a happier, more spiritual life, by giving you insights and teachings in their own areas of expertise. Joshua shares philosophy, Dr John discusses healing and Pierre gives guidance on healing of the planet. Just a sample of the topics included.

How do you tell if Spirit is communicating or if it is man? Feel the words as you read. Man can inspire but Spirit's voice goes deeper than the mind. It nourishes the soul, resonates with the heart and gives an overwhelming feeling of love.

Uniquely in this fascinating book Bob queries and challenges the teachings given rather than blindly accepting them as the truth because they come from Spirit. There are many levels of truth in spirit just as there are on earth. The more knowledgeable or specialised the teacher the higher the level of truth. Think of primary school and college. The basic information is given in primary school but more detailed and complex understandings at college. So it is with spirit guides. They all have a basic understanding of truths, but there are many wonderful Spirit teachers out there who come forward to teach higher spiritual teachings when the appropriate medium is found to allow them an outlet.

Everyone's journey is different, beliefs are unique to us but I can honestly say that when I read the manuscript I was amazed at its power to inspire and heal. As you read this book your spirit guide will be close and help you understand the teachings that are relevant to you.

Anne Lewis, ICHF, Min ICSP
East Riding of Yorkshire, England

ACKNOWLEDGEMENTS

I wish to express my thanks to four people in particular who have encouraged me in the writing of this book. Namely, Anne Lewis who is a spiritual medium and healer, Peter John who is a psychic artist, Carter Nelson a friend that I have known for over forty years, and Michael Luxford a fellow 'Camphiller'.

I asked each of them to read the manuscript and give me their honest comments and feedback. I am very grateful that they found time to do this, and I have taken their comments on board in the final draft.

My thanks also to Philip Clarkson and Dorothy Lee and to the rest of the team at 'Author House' for facilitating the publishing of this book, and to Hazel Townsley who typed the manuscript for me – in record time! Also to Neil Castleton for our fascinating clairvoyant research-sessions.

However, above all, I thank those friends in Spirit who have willingly cooperated in providing me with the main contents of this book and who expressed their clear wish to see this published and available for others to read. Indeed while on a morning walk in February 2018, I told one of my Guides that I still had not found the right publisher for my manuscript. That afternoon I was attracted to a book which, I then discovered, had been published by Author House and also contained their telephone number. Thereby, my initial contact with Mr Clarkson that same day. So I am very grateful for your guidance and your trust in me to convey what you all wish to share at this time.

Whilst thus fully acknowledging your inputs as Guides, as the writer of this book I am the one who carries overall responsibility for its publication in this form.

SYNOPSIS

The book has twelve chapters:

1. Introduction. Describes something of the background which has led to the writing of this book.
2. Methodology. Describes how I communicate with Spirit Guides, my state of consciousness, and the development of trust and confidence in this process.
3. The Guides. Gives an introduction to each of the Guides in turn, from what I know, and what they say themselves. Each Guide will take on a Chapter, give 'Teachings', and also participate in a 'Question and Answer' session with me.
4. Joshua. Gives his teachings which serve as a good introduction to the position of Guides and the need for a new outlook, based on a truly spiritual perception of ourselves and the World.
5. Dr John. Gives teachings specifically geared to promoting good health. (Very relevant nowadays when various health issues and lifestyle choices hit the headlines almost daily.) A first mention of 'karma and reincarnation' in the Q&A session with him.
6. Markos. His teachings point to the source of true Wisdom in our own hearts, and he refers to the activities of prayer and meditation. (There is much interest in 'mindfulness meditation' nowadays.)
7. Red Cloud. He talks about us each having a chosen 'mission' in our lives, which we have decided upon before birth. Everything

has meaning and purpose in our lives. Spirit Guides can help us if called upon.

8. <u>Raja Lampa</u>. He points to Spirit deep within each human soul, and urges us to connect to our true spirit selves, through meditation and contemplation. He says the Spirit World is ready to help us in this.

9. <u>Pierre</u>. Brings in the perspective of the health and well-being of the whole planet. (A very topical concern nowadays.) A new sense of responsibility and respect is needed, and to learn to cooperate with spiritual beings.

10. <u>Pan</u>. Continues the theme of the health of the planet, of Mother Earth. Harmony between the different Kingdoms of Nature. We need to learn to cooperate with nature spirits and elemental beings. Human beings as 'custodians' of the Earth.

11. <u>Philip</u>. Speaks from the side of the 'Guardian Angel', which each of us have. All beings on a path of evolution. The universe teems with life and consciousness. We are only limited by our set beliefs and expectations.

12. <u>Reflective Review</u>. I identify some key 'themes' from the various teachings and discuss them.

1

INTRODUCTION

In 2007 my book ***Spirit Communications*** was published. My purpose in writing it at that time was to share some of the communications which I believed I had received from Spirit Guides and also from my family in spirit. Thereby to demonstrate that it is possible to establish such rapport. I hoped this might encourage others who wished to communicate with those in spirit, by exploring their own capacities for doing so. However, the book mainly described my own particular path, or journey, of development in learning to engage in such two-way conversations.

I shared quite frankly and openly my own trepidations and uncertainties in exploring, what for me, was new terrain. The ongoing search for certainty and validity in this area of research was really a red thread running through the book. Not for nothing was one of the chapters entitled, 'A Doubting Thomas'! The book would never have been written were it not for the fact that in December 2004 I wrote to Anne Lewis, a spiritual medium, to request a postal Reading from her. I did this mainly to see if I would gain confirmation of the authenticity of my abilities as a Spiritual Healer.

This confirmation was given, unequivocally, at the beginning of the Reading which I received early in the New Year in January 2005. Anne stated,

> 'As I tune into your photograph and tune into your letter I see a spirit doctor stood behind you in a three-quarter length white coat and dark trousers, and he has a round face. I cannot see his hair very clearly so I cannot determine if he hasn't got a lot of hair or I am unable to see it. He is directly behind you and he wishes to work with you in spiritual healing.'

Interestingly, in an earlier book entitled ***Spirit Healing***, I had already discussed the notion of spirit guides and, in particular, so called 'spirit doctors' within the context of spiritual healing practice. This was some time before I first became consciously aware of my own Spirit Doctor, through Anne, in 2005. In that earlier publication I had acknowledged that many healers believed, or knew, that they were helped and guided in their work by friends across the threshold. That is to say, beings acting from out of the spiritual world. These could be discarnate human souls and/or highly evolved beings belonging to the ranks of the spiritual hierarchies, such as angels and archangels. Moreover, I also pointed out that already in the early part of the 20th century, the Austrian spiritual-researcher Rudolf Steiner had clearly indicated that there should come about in future a much more conscious and active participation between us and those who had died. Therefore, although the concept of 'Spirit Guides' may be strongly associated in some people's minds with the traditions of Spiritualism and mediumship, I believe this to be a far too narrow perspective nowadays.

I continued to ask for regular Readings from Anne and, in the third of these, the spirit doctor who had apparently been working with me already for some years introduced himself as Dr John Cahill (though Anne was not sure of the spelling). He told something of his background and professional interests (in that former lifetime) and then went on to state that he and I could communicate without the services of the medium. I decided to take up this offer, and challenge, by practising 'sitting in the silence' as he had suggested. By the time I received the fourth Reading from Anne, about a month later, I was also made aware of another Guide in spirit who was linked with me. His name was Joshua Isaiah and his task was as a teacher. Anne wrote, 'He is there to answer your questions and queries on spirit matters and philosophy.'

In the course of the communications which I received from these two new friends in spirit a main theme repeatedly emerged, namely the need for me to develop trust in myself and in my abilities, and also in them. Gradually, step by tentative step, this trust began to unfold and to grow stronger.

Now, in 2017, and ten years on from *Spirit Communications*, I have the impulse at the age of 70 to once again put pen to paper. However, this time to share with readers not so much my particular path of inner development, but rather to give my Guides in spirit (who have recently increased in number) the opportunity to express themselves directly. I invited them to author their own chapters, which

I received telepathically and wrote down. Thereby they can share with us the teachings which they consider relevant and important at this time. I was therefore willing to be an awake and conscious 'channel' for these communications. In addition to the teachings per se, I thought it important to be able to ask them questions about these contents. They willingly agreed to this request and so I put questions to them which, I can imagine, any open-minded, thinking readers would also want to ask. Perhaps also to challenge what the Guides have asserted. Each chapter is therefore structured so that the 'teachings' are first given and then the 'question and answer' sessions follow on with each Guide in turn.

Exactly how these communications were received by me is described in the following chapter on 'Methodology'. This will also refer back to the beginnings of this process which started some twelve years ago. In the final chapter I offer a 'Reflective Review' of the teachings and identify some main themes emerging from them. However I recommend that readers reflect on these things for themselves and see whether the contents per se make sense to them. Are there helpful, constructive thoughts to take on board, to live with, and see if they bring a greater sense of meaning or purpose into your own life? Or, put simply, do they ring true to you? If they do, then you may feel that the one who purports to have given these teachings is more than a figment of my own imagination, perhaps indeed a genuine person, or being, living in a different dimension than our physical, material realm.

To be open to such possibilities may be the key required for you, yourself, to begin conscious rapport with your own Guides in spirit? But, whatever you do, always bear clearly in mind that true Guides will never seek to impose their will on yours. They will only advise if asked to and never attempt to steer you into any direction that is not of your own choosing. Freedom of thinking and freedom of the will (yours) is, I believe, a prerequisite for any genuine spirit dialogue and cooperation. Anything less than this is, in my opinion, utterly unacceptable and is to be avoided. It is essential for you to maintain good health and especially a free and balanced mind.

I realise of course that in publishing this book I also run the risk of laying myself wide open to ridicule. There will be sceptics who say that this book is nothing other than self-deception and that while I may have convinced myself of the authenticity of 'Guides' and their 'messages', there is really no sound basis for this conviction. I can very well understand this sceptical and critical viewpoint. In my book **Spirit Communications** I also struggled to clarify these matters to myself and to understand what 'trusting in myself and in Spirit' really meant. So I would simply suggest to those of you who remain sceptical, or even suspicious, of the notion of 'Spirit Guides' per se that you see whether the *actual content* of the chapters, irrespective of their alleged spirit sources, rings true to you. Do you agree with me that an open-minded approach is often, if not always, more constructive and fruitful for us than a closed and therefore biased mind?

Certainly we live in an exciting time when spirituality is an important and emergent theme across various professions and walks of life. It is a theme which underpins much popular literature that covers such subjects as: the chakras; the human energy field or aura; near-death experiences; spiritual healing; psychic development; mediumship; channelling; past-life regression; angel experiences; mindfulness meditation; etc. etc. The prevalence of the new, open, spirituality today, contrasts strongly with the times in which Rudolf Steiner wrote and lectured one hundred or so years ago. However, the wide range and choice of publications and practices calls, I think, for both an open-minded and also a critically-thinking and informed approach. It is often good to compare and contrast what different authors and spiritual teachers put forward, and see if they validate each other or show significant divergences.

However, the very popularity of such resources does clearly suggest that many people in our mainly materialistic culture are actively seeking for a deeper sense of purpose, meaning, and value in their lives. It has become my own firm belief that Spirit Guides also wish to help us, in freedom and love, in this modern, or postmodernist, self-knowledge quest.

2

METHODOLOGY

How on earth did these communications from alleged Spirit Guides come through? What methods, techniques, or devices were used and, in particular, what state of consciousness was I in at the time? These questions, which are all to do with methodology, are essential to address if the chapters which follow are to be taken seriously.

To begin to answer these questions I will refer back to the fourth Reading which I had from Anne Lewis in April 2005. I asked her then what sort of communication I could have with Dr John in terms of method rather than contents. Anne replied,

> 'He says that as you are a mentally active person he will be able to access this area for communication and you will be able to hear his voice in your head. Do not be impatient with this because his thoughts will be in your voice, not his. You will have to be aware of your thoughts to determine which are his words and which are yours.'

Therefore the essential feature of this form of mental rapport was for me to be clearly aware of my own thoughts, as expressed in words, vis a vis the thoughts I would receive independently from Dr John. Interestingly, the core question of 'Where do thoughts actually come from, and mine in particular?' had been a recurrent issue for me, probably since childhood. What, I wondered, is the source, or sources, of all those diverse thoughts and images which relentlessly course through our inner mental landscapes, sometimes with unwanted chaos and confusion? In reference to Dr John, Anne added,

> 'He himself is a more mentally orientated person and as such your communications will be mainly by clairaudience.'

Well, the term that I use in describing this method to myself and others is 'telepathy' in the sense of receiving thoughts from another, rather than clairaudience. I mean telepathic thoughts expressed in language, rather than any particular sensations, feelings or emotions.

I do not hear John's voice, nor that of any other Guides, in my head, but I certainly do receive communications in English in my mind.

For clarity I should state that I do not enter into any sort of trance or semi-conscious mental condition when communing with those in Spirit. I am in my normal awake state of mind and fully aware of myself. Indeed as a thinking person I have no wish to enter into any dream-like or trance state, although I am aware that some mediums do work whilst in trance. This is their choice but it is not my way. I have never been involved with Spiritualism, nor have I taken part in so-called psychic 'development circles' as have many well-known mediums. On the other hand I am somewhat familiar with the inner activity of meditation and have been a regular daily meditator for the past 36 years, though in saying this I am not claiming that I yet know how to really meditate deeply. An older friend of mine once described meditation as the ability to be fully there in the present. This is not at all easy to achieve! However this is a subject which we do not need to explore further in the present context, save to say that learning to become inwardly silent and alert is a prerequisite for my meditation practice.

Initially, and then for some years, I always wrote down the communications I received from friends in Spirit as they were being given. For example I still have nine A4 bound notebooks in which there is a record of the communications which I received over two years and nine months, from the end of February 2006 to mid-December 2008. In the book **Spirit Communications** Anne Lewis's eight Readings for me covered the period January 2005 to January 2006, whilst some of my own early contacts, also published in that book, were spread over the nine months from July 2005 to March 2006.

All that was required for me to link up with those in Spirit was to sit myself down with that clear intention in mind and become quiet and receptive. What Dr John calls 'sitting in the silence'. Then, in reply to a question that I would put, thoughts and words would flow into my mind and I would commit them to paper. My main contacts were with Joshua for teachings or advice and with John for matters to do with spiritual healing. However, looking through the nine notebooks, there are also to be found some communications from my deceased parents; from my niece's son Mathew who, aged eleven, died from cancer in 2006; from my maternal grandparents; from Philip my Guardian Angel, as well as several others. (I can well imagine that by now some readers may feel somewhat bemused and incredulous.) In all cases there was a clear telepathic line of articulate conversation between us, rather like having a telephone call, and always initiated by me. It is important to say that I have never felt imposed upon by any Spirit sources but experience such interchange as a direct response to my own free enquiries. Essentially this form of inner rapport has more or less continued over the past twelve years. The main change is that nowadays, and already for some years, I often verbally speak out loud the communications which I am receiving instead of always writing them down. There is also no set time or place for such conversations but they happen as and when I initiate them, say on a walk in the countryside, or to do some shopping, or even whilst driving in the car! (Just as you might talk to a passenger.) This has become like second nature to me, though naturally I don't make a habit of this when other people are around, for obvious reasons!

The teachings and conversations given in this book were of course written down verbatim since they were intended to stand as chapters from their respective spirit authors. In order to receive these contents I sat down in my room at a regular time each morning over a period of eighteen days, from 22 May to 8 June 2017. By keeping to this daily commitment I showed a clear willingness to receive whatever the Guides wished to bring through for the book. These sessions normally lasted up to one hour. As in all spiritual work it is very important to have a clear intentionality and motivation. The core of this intentionality is that whatever we do is ethical, and for the highest good, rather than being egotistical and for our own vanity!

On each occasion the thoughts flowed effortlessly with just an occasional pause to coin the correct word. In sequence of time the 'teachings' were first received from all the Guides and then, a week or so later, I asked questions to each of them about what they had said. For the sake of transparency it should be mentioned that I did not need to sit in any particular posture, nor to engage in any meditative or concentration exercises, or any special breathing rhythms. I just sat naturally at my bureau as I would in order to write a letter. The only difference between writing a letter and writing the communications was that I would sometimes have a brief shaking, or vibrating, of my upper body from the waist upwards. This is something which has happened for years and to which I am completely accustomed. It also often happens when I practise sitting in the silence or for meditation. Why does it occur at all? I tend to think that these physical movements have something to do with increasing my own vibrational energy levels within my auric field. (My hands also often shake when I hold crystals.) However, this phenomenon does not affect my self-awareness nor my thinking. It is just one of those things and may be peculiar to me? Recently, in March 2018, I asked Joshua whether this bodily shaking was indeed a way of increasing my auric energy levels. He said that it was rather the other way around. When my auric frequencies were raised then my body responded accordingly.

Perhaps it would be appropriate to describe what I do as 'channelling' and various books have been published with channelled contents from alleged spirit sources. In all such cases I think it is important to know the state of consciousness of the recipient. Why is this important if the actual contents seem reasonable? Because I value fully conscious co-operative participation with Spirit rather than any dimmed-down involvement which might be more vulnerable to control and manipulation. This is however my viewpoint and should not be taken as criticism of any particular 'trance-mediums' for example.

I am not a 'medium' given that their main function is to bring through evidence of after-death survival, nor do I consider myself a 'clairvoyant' or 'a sensitive'. I do however see myself as a 'questioner and researcher', as evidenced in my various university-based projects along qualitative methods of enquiry. Over the past twelve years and as an integral factor in the field of spirit-research I have developed a stronger trust in my own ability to communicate with those in Spirit and particularly with the Guides I have come to know well through frequent contact. To learn to trust in oneself and one's Guides is not the same as showing naive blind belief. It is far more an inner attitude which grows through the test of time and is supported by the helpful advice and guidance which has been received. Both Joshua and Dr John have continued to give advice and support over the past twelve years, whilst always respecting my own choices and decisions. Having said this, there have also been times when the information received from them did not appear to be accurate or correct. What I received was not borne out by the actual facts. When such discrepancies occur there may be a number of possible explanations for them. The one that I have considered most likely was that, at those times, I did not channel properly what the Guides were communicating. However this immediately begs the question, 'How could this occur?' Perhaps through some lack of synchronisation of energies between myself and the Guide? In this regard the following contact with Joshua in August 2014 is worth including here.

*****

Bob   Joshua can you explain to me how our telepathic communications work, and am I correct to call them telepathy?

Joshua   Bob my friend, yes you are correct to call them telepathic communications since I speak directly into your mind. How do they work? Well, quite simply, I attune myself with your energies on a mental level and give you my thoughts. It's as simple as that my friend. It is purely a matter of attunement and of tuning-in to each other. Just as you tune a radio to receive a certain radio station, so you and I tune-in to each other. Since this can be done immediately, communication also comes about at once and quite effortlessly. Once the channel (you) has been opened to receive, then the giving of the communication is very easy. This is how it works from mind to mind. All depends on the synchronising of the energies and frequencies. Once that's effected the communication flows through easily and unimpeded.

Bob   Well, Joshua, I accept that we can easily tune-in, but how is that if I bring through others, say John or Mathew?

Joshua   My friend it is exactly the same, no different. You just both (or more) tune-in and the thoughts flow in between. As easy as that.

Bob   Well, what about if I speak with Philip, as an Angel being?

Joshua   Again, no different my friend. It all depends on being able to tune-in.

Bob   Thank you Joshua.

*****

The immediacy of being able to tune-in, which Joshua refers to, is by now part of my normal daily experience. If, for example, my niece calls me on the telephone from where she lives in North London and asks for specific advice from her deceased son, then I simply put the request to him and pass on the message I receive.

I would say that if any information gleaned from Spirit can be checked for accuracy, then it should be. Guides are not omniscient or infallible. Nonetheless the advice and guidance that I have received for myself, and sometimes others, has proved to be very helpful, practical and reassuring. Real-life situations and circumstances are ever changing and mobile and open to a variety of influences. Therefore advice received at one point of time may differ from that which is most appropriate either before or later. This can apply to individual health issues as much as to human relationships and challenges. These realities therefore need to be borne in mind, both when receiving and acting upon any advice or guidance received from Spirit Guides.

Although I have now described my own way of tuning-in to my Guides in order to be a clear channel for telepathic communications with them, there are further questions to raise concerning what has been given through this means. The most important of these is of course, 'How can we be sure that the information, or teachings, are true?' This same question applies in fact to **all** such channelled, or inspired, contents derived from alleged spirit sources. Are there ways in which we can test the validity and credibility of what has been thus received and communicated? If not, then many may argue that it really comes down to a matter of personal belief or disbelief, of subjective acceptance or rejection.

I think there are a number of approaches for testing such teachings. For example, if we are able to examine and compare the information given from different, independent, sources do we find agreement and consistency? Such a comparison could be done via a literature search of published works by different mediums, psychics, clairvoyants or channellers. This would certainly be an interesting academic study to conduct. Whilst agreements, both in general and with regard to particular points, could well increase our sense of reliability and confidence in the findings, it would not necessarily provide irrefutable proof. Nonetheless, such published 'evidence' might be compelling and convincing enough for many of us? Let me also add that as a lifelong student of Rudolf Steiner's anthroposophy, or Spiritual-Science, I do find therein many confirmations of what the Guides are alluding to.

Another approach is instead of just relying on the information given by others, to try to establish our own conscious contact with our Guides and thereby receive direct experiences. I think it is particularly interesting that in this present book I have been able to give teachings from not one, but from eight Guides. As later mentioned, I had the impression that a 'Circle of Guides' were making themselves known to me in order to offer their own contributions. Do we therefore find mutual support and coherence in what they have to say, or are they at loggerheads with one another? I leave you to come to your own informed conclusions on this point.

Yet another approach is to apply to our own lives and activities, any practical suggestions or advice given from Spirit sources. We can then see if this really works for us. A small yet significant example of this is the advice given by Pan in Chapter 10, to take care of our local surroundings by picking up litter. I have applied this advice and have on several occasions gone out with a big bag to collect the assorted rubbish on the housing estate where I live, as well as nearby. There is undoubtedly a totally different feel to the area when it is de-littered, and I can well imagine that the environmental energies are changed for the better. This is also a very simple way of helping to do one's bit for the planet! Steiner made extensive researches into the spiritual dimensions, and his findings underpin many very practical activities, including; education, medicine, biodynamic agriculture, social renewal, etc. etc.

Whenever possible, a combination of such approaches may well provide a good means for testing out spirit teachings, and also testing the findings of spiritual researchers such as Steiner. Clearly it is important to do our best to ascertain the reliability, veracity, and validity of such contents, rather than just accept them at face value. However, our own intuitions and feeling for truth can also play an important part in this evaluation process.

I hope I have in this chapter made my methodology for receiving 'the communications' contained in this book crystal clear! The relevant chapters flowed through my mind, to being expressed in writing, very easily. Much more so than this and other chapters that I have had to think through myself! Whilst I have already pointed out that in all spiritual work it is important to have a clear ethical intentionality, this does not mean that we need to be somehow morally 'perfect' before daring to get to know our Spirit Guides. I am daily confronted by my own inadequacies and shortcomings. My own spiritual awareness and development is, I think, best described as, 'a work in progress', albeit slowly! The Guides are there to give us their support and encouragement, not to condemn or judge us. I believe that work with them should strengthen, in a healthy way, our own self-empowerment and confidence and in no way undermine these positive attributes. A good sense of humour is also very helpful, particularly when directed towards oneself. The many conversations that I've had with my clairvoyant friend Neil over the years always involved some laughter and merriment.

Finally I should like to just mention some research which I did in receiving, not thoughts or concepts, but pictures and images from Spirit. This work was done with Joshua in June/July 2016 through daily contact over a period of six weeks. The contact consisted of 45 lessons with Joshua (all recorded in an A4 notebook) in each of which I endeavoured to make myself receptive to the images sent through. I found this a much greater challenge than distinguishing my own thoughts from those of others. We are almost continually surrounded, and sometimes bombarded, by images of all kinds. Images in daily life and images from the media, television in particular. We have also countless memory images. To learn to make the mind blank, like a clear screen on which to receive pictures given from Spirit is, certainly for me, a difficult task. It was another learning process to add to the methodology of ***Spirit Communications***. Next we will turn to the Guides themselves.

3

THE GUIDES

When I had the thought to write this chapter I asked my Guide, Joshua, what he advised.

*****

Bob   Joshua do you think it a good idea if I let each of the Guides introduce themselves to the readers of this book, rather than me putting down what prior information I have? What do you think?

Joshua   My friend, we would suggest that you do both. Put down whatever knowledge you have, as well as letting us speak for ourselves. All blessings, Joshua and the others.

Bob   Okay, I will ask Joshua, John, Markos, Red Cloud, Raja Lampa, Pierre, Pan and Philip to introduce themselves and I may then also add whatever I otherwise know of them. I will ask each in turn if they can do this.

*****

However, on reflection, it seemed to me better to first record something of my prior knowledge of the Guides, before setting down their own introductions to readers. This is then in keeping with the actual time sequence of my own awareness of their 'appearances' in my life. So, beginning with:

JOSHUA

As I have already mentioned in the 'Introduction' I first became aware of Joshua through my friend Anne Lewis. In the fourth Reading which I received from Anne in April 2005 she wrote:

'As I am saying this I am being shown a Jewish cap – it is one of your guides who is acknowledging what I have just said.

He is a Jewish elder and he is now showing me a ceremonial either apron or sash that he would wear in the synagogue as part of his uniform. ... He is encouraging you to make your sitting time a regular thing so that spirits know when they can come and teach you.'

In the following Reading a month later Anne wrote:

'As I sat and asked your doctor to come close to answer your questions, it was the learned gentleman who answered – the Jewish elder. He said that whilst Dr John was around you for the healing there were other guides who were with you more often. One of them is himself and he is there to answer your questions and queries on spirit matters and philosophy.'

The contact and communications which I then had with Joshua are given in my book **Spirit Communications** and interested readers may wish to look at these. However I have maintained a close relationship with Joshua since then and right up to the present day. In that sense he is my main Spirit Guide, to whom I turn when I have questions which are not specifically to do with healing. My understanding is that I have a long relationship with Joshua which goes back into previous incarnations. Now however is his own current introduction to you.

INTRODUCTION

Joshua   Shalom, my friends. My name is Joshua Isaiah.

This is the name which I bore in my former life on Earth when I lived and worked as a Jewish Rabbi and teacher. It is the name that people knew me as and it is the name by which Bob knows me in our communications.
I would like to describe what my task is in Spirit Worlds. Fundamentally I am given the task of teaching, of teaching

19

those on Earth who wish to come into communication with those in Spirit. This is my central task and it is one I have undertaken with Bob and which, to this day, I continue to undertake with him. With Bob, as it can also often be with others, it has been a question of establishing a relationship of trust and faith in himself and also in me. When I say trust and faith I am not asking for any sort of 'blind faith', but a faith that is borne out of knowledge. Knowledge which arises through continued communication and practice.

'Practice makes perfect' is the saying which expresses that, through continued regular efforts, an ability is acquired which enables a certain proficiency at a task. It is to be of assistance to those who seek spiritual proficiency, who seek to develop their own inherent spiritual abilities, that I devote my own time and efforts. It is a task I am given in the realm of Spirit and one that I do most willingly. I am no longer bound of course by the particular religious teachings which I practised in my last earthly incarnation. No, I now have a much broader and wider area of expertise shall I say, and it is applied to each individual who comes into contact with me and asks for my help and assistance.

So this my friends is the role which I undertake from Spirit, for the benefit of those on Earth who wish to become my pupils, so to speak. But of course I mean 'pupils' in the freest possible way, since we are equals in our spiritual essence and I do not profess to know more than they. I only help them to discover what they already know in their deepest being, but are still unaware of in their ordinary consciousness. Perhaps this is sufficient as an introduction to all who may read this book? Shalom, shalom, **Joshua Isaiah**.

Bob   Thank you Joshua.

DR JOHN

As I have already explained I became aware of John in the very first Reading which Anne Lewis did for me, when, as she tuned into my photograph and letter she wrote:

'I see a spirit doctor stood behind you in a three-quarter length white coat and dark trousers, and he has a round face.'

When, two months later, I asked Anne for further information about John, she wrote:

'For the purposes of this enquiry my name is Dr John Cahill ['I am not sure of the spelling' wrote Anne.] I was born in Michigan in the USA. I was of peasant stock you would say and I was one of the first in my family to graduate with a doctorate. My life mainly dealt with psychiatry and its relevant social consequences.'

He went on to describe that he now works through healers, together with other spirit doctors. In answer to my question as to how long John had been working with me, he answered, 'I have been around you in a concrete way for around five years,' ie. this was very soon after I began my training as a Spiritual Healer in January 1999. Various communications with John concerning my/our healing practice are contained in the book **Spirit Communications**, but this is an ongoing relationship and I frequently request healing help for those in need of it. Now however is his own introduction for you.

INTRODUCTION

Bob   So John, can I now ask you to introduce yourself to readers?

John   Yes my friend, you can.

When I lived on Earth in my last lifetime I was a medical doctor. I lived in the USA and I practised there around my home town. I was mainly centred in Illinois, in this area of the country. However the important thing to say concerns my present work in Spirit, rather than my past work on Earth.

My task is to work with healers on Earth, specifically 'Spiritual Healers', that is to say those who are willing and able to channel through the healing energies which are directed by myself and my colleagues in Spirit. We work as a team with the healers who are willing to cooperate with us. Of course it does not always happen that the healers are exactly aware of who we are. It is quite sufficient if they allow the healing energies to pass through them to their patients or clients. However there will also be some healers, and Bob is one of these, who are very aware of who they are working with in Spirit.

The term 'Spirit Doctors' is sometimes used for us and we do consider this to be an apt term. We are able to be especially effective if the healers we work with can tune into us easily and allow the energies which we send to meet the specific needs of individual patients to flow through easily. The less the person gets in the way, so to speak, the better it is for us and our patients. So this is my specific task. It is an impulse which I carried with me into Spirit, following my last death on Earth, and I am happy that I am allowed to continue with my vocation on this side of life.

I think this is all that I need to say in order to introduce myself to our readers. **Dr John.**

Bob   Thank you John.

MARKOS

I first became aware of Markos, as one of my Spirit Guides, through my contact with the psychic artist Peter John, whom I met at a local *Mind, Body, Spirit Fair* in October 2016. On that occasion I wanted to ask Peter John for a Reading and Portrait, but he was booked out already. Therefore I asked him for a postal Reading instead and I received this and the portrait of Markos in early November 2016. Peter John gave me a very informative Reading and I would like to share with you what he had to say about Markos.

> 'I saw Markos very clearly when using my mind's eye to show me a picture of your Spirit Guide. The picture of him was clear to me and he reminded me of Archbishop Makarios. Markos identified himself to me as Greek and a monk. He lived, as he shows himself in the portrait, around 1200AD. This was a time of great change in the Byzantine Empire, but his firm Christian beliefs helped him through troubled times. He was able to live with very little material needs and encouraged and prayed for others to be more frugal and make their way in life peacefully and with humility. He is clearly very wise. I have picked up that he is a philosopher and is greatly revered in the Spirit World. He is a high soul and works with you at the highest level.'

Peter John went on to describe my relationship with Markos and then added as a postscript,

> 'Markos hails from Thessalonika in Greece and of a more sophisticated Christian Byzantine background. A man who pacified and paved the way for other lesser men to make trading possible between them. Markos was a man of the people and on the whole was greatly loved.'

The portrait of Markos now hangs on a wall in my bedroom, together with paintings of some of my other Guides.

The communication which I myself received from Markos is now given below.

INTRODUCTION

Bob   Well Markos, would you also like to now introduce yourself to our readers?

Markos   Yes my friend, I would.

I was born in Greece and I lived in the 17th/18th centuries in the area around present day Turkey, near the Black Sea area. I was a merchant by profession but I was also a philosopher. I was known locally for my teachings and I did have a following of some disciples or pupils. Not that I set out to have such followers, but they nonetheless came towards me because of what I was able to teach them.

In Spirit I have also the task to help enlighten, through knowledge and understanding, those who are drawn towards me. When I say I have this task in Spirit, I also mean with this that I can come into communication with those in the Earth sphere who wish to gain knowledge and understanding of spiritual dimensions. Therefore my task is mainly as a teacher, as someone who can be of service in this particular way. I do not work alone, none of us do in Spirit, but I belong to a particular group of 'people' shall I say, spiritually speaking, who also have such teaching responsibilities. We work together to help those who come into contact with us. Therefore my relationship with Bob is as a teacher to a pupil, in the sense that, like any good teacher, I try to be of service to my pupils. Perhaps this is sufficient as an introduction? All blessings, **Markos.**

Now, as readers will have noticed, there appears to be an obvious discrepancy regarding the dates of Markos's life on Earth, between Peter John's Reading and my own communication with Markos. This was something that I therefore queried.

Bob   Markos you have said here, if I've got it right, that you lived in the 17th/18th centuries, ie. the 1600/1700 hundreds AD. Now Peter John told me you lived around 1200, ie. the 13th century. So how is this? Has he or I got it wrong?

Markos   No, neither of you have it wrong. In fact you are both right. I lived in Greece in two incarnations, not one, and in my Introduction I have referred to the last one, rather than the former.

Bob   Markos, I do wonder if I have got this information incorrectly, since Peter John seemed to be very clear in what he wrote to me.

Markos   No, you don't have it wrong. It is as I say that we are here referring to two incarnations in the same, or similar, geographical area on Earth. Please do not doubt your own abilities, but trust in your abilities to channel such communications soundly.

Bob   Okay. Thank you. I'll have to think on this further.

Although my understanding regarding reincarnation is that, generally, subsequent lifetimes tend to take place in different areas and cultures on Earth in order to provide the soul with different sorts of learning situations, perhaps this is not always the case. Indeed I can imagine that over a time-period of some five hundred or so years, earthly conditions may have changed considerably so that the incarnating soul can glean quite new and fresh experiences.

At any event I wish to keep an open mind on this matter.

RED CLOUD

The way in which I became aware of Red Cloud as another of my Spirit Guides is particularly interesting – at least to me!

You will recall that near the end of Chapter 2 on Methodology, I mentioned that I had experimented in receiving images from Spirit in addition to thoughts and words. I first did this, systematically, in June/July 2016 over a period of about six weeks. However I decided to resume this image-receiving work in March 2017 with the support of both Joshua and Markos. This is not the place to describe in detail how this work proceeded, suffice it to say that a wide variety of pictures came into my mind over the following month. Amongst these were some very clear scenes set in North America in the days of the Red Indians. During that particular time in early March 2017 when I saw these inner scenarios I also had during the day the image of an Indian face arising in my mind. This went on for some days. So, puzzled by this, and whilst pushing my young grandson in his pram, I asked Joshua about the Indian face that I saw in my mind's eye. Joshua told me that his name was 'Red Cloud' and that he was another of my Guides. Apparently Red Cloud would be happy to work with Joshua and Markos in the picture-receiving activities we were then doing.

Now I had no idea at that time whether Red Cloud was a bona-fide Indian name. I certainly had no recollection of hearing it before. Well, about an hour or so later I was again pushing my grandson in his pram and looked in a charity shop that I often frequented. I glanced at the second-hand books and one of them immediately caught my eye. It had a bright red cover and when I picked it off the shelf I read that it was entitled *The Inconvenient Indian*. It was all about native American Indians! When I brought the book home with me and looked at the index I found the name 'Red Cloud'. So, sheer coincidence or clear guidance?

I asked my wife to look up the name 'Red Cloud' on the internet and, when she did so, I discovered that he was a well-known leader, a Chief of the Sioux. I therefore turned to him and asked,

Bob   Red Cloud, can you tell me if you were that famous Indian leader, or have you perhaps the same name but were/are a different individual?

Red Cloud "How" my friend. Yes I was that famous Indian leader who later, as you say, became a Christian. In Spirit it is who we are as a spirit that counts, rather than who we were on Earth.

Well, this is the true tale of how I became aware of Red Cloud as another of my Spirit Guides. I will let him give his own introduction to you.

INTRODUCTION

Bob   Red Cloud, are you ready and willing to introduce yourself to readers?

Red Cloud Yes, I am both ready and willing my friend, let us start.

I was a Chief of the Sioux in my last incarnation on Earth. It was then my task, my self-appointed task, to try to bring a peaceful resolution between the White men and the Red Indians. There were those who could not understand why I took this view. They wanted me to be much more proactive for the Sioux and others, but I felt that peace was more important than war. So I tried to be a peacemaker.

In Spirit my task is also to do all I can, from this side of life, to help bring peace and blessing to the Earth and to humanity. I am no longer bound by my former affiliations and blood relationships. I can now act more independently from my tribal or racial concerns. So I wish to be a peacemaker in a much more global sense and to do all I can to bring about reconciliation and understanding among the Nations. This is the task for which I work from Spirit, not alone of course, but with many others who want World-peace and World-harmony. Perhaps this is sufficient to introduce myself?

Bob   Red Cloud, why did you make yourself known to me, and why do you want to contribute to this book?

Red Cloud I made myself known to you Bob for the very reason that I wanted to contribute to this unique book. It is important that people realise that we in Spirit want to work with them to bring peace to Earth and to avoid conflict and wars.

Bob   Thank you.

Postscript:

Exactly a month after I had become aware of Red Cloud through being given that name to the Indian face by Joshua, I met Peter John once more at the local *Mind, Body, Spirit Fair.* I told him of my experiences with meeting Red Cloud.

In the Reading which we had, Peter John described seeing an Indian on a beautiful white-grey horse, high up on the rocks, holding out a lance as a last gesture. Peter John referred to, 'Man's ability to overcome his own vanity'. Asking, 'Is that the position of strength?' 'Has he made a momentous, correct decision for his people?' 'Would they stand up for peace, against the image that it is stronger to fight than be peaceful?'

The portrait that he did for me on this occasion was that of a young-looking Red Indian with, to my mind, a rather serious and sad expression on his face. Later on that day I asked Red Cloud if the drawing was a good likeness of himself. He replied,

Red Cloud "How" my friend, yes it is a good likeness of how I presented myself to the artist today. But remember, it is simply a likeness, an image which can help you relate to me as a Being. Images, even of yourself, change with time. From childhood to youth, to old age. It is a changing image, but the Being, the essential Being, remains the same. So take the image as a means to an end, to relating to me per se.

*****

I had the feeling, the impression, that Guides were coming forward as it were, making themselves known to me, because they wanted to contribute to the book I intended to write. It was as if a 'Circle of Guides' was around me. The 'Introductions' which now follow on bear witness to their wish to participate in the contents of the book.

RAJA LAMPA

It is likely that guidance from Spirit can come in various ways. For example, being prompted to pick up and read a particular book at a certain time. I have long had an interest in the books of His Holiness the Dalai Lama. Altogether, stories to do with Tibet have had a certain fascination for me, no doubt partly fuelled by the series of books written by one 'Lobsang Rampa' which were published in the 1950s, 1960s and 1970s. The first book from Rampa entitled *The Third Eye* in which he purported to describe his childhood and upbringing in Tibet and culminating in his becoming a Tibetan Lama, captured the imagination of many spiritually-seeking souls like myself. It later emerged that, apparently, the writer of these popular books was said to be a 'Cyril Henry Hoskin' who had never set foot in Tibet and who adopted the pen-name of Lobsang Rampa. Whatever the truth may be, his literary creations certainly helped to put mysterious Tibet firmly on the map for many Westerners. In contrast to any possible fiction, the account of Tibet and Lhasa contained in the book by Heinrich Harrer entitled *Seven Years in Tibet* provided fascinating insights into this largely inaccessible country and its spirituality. Harrer's authenticity was confirmed through his personal friendship with the Dalai Lama.

So, like others no doubt, I have had a great interest in Tibet and in the increasing number of books produced by, or on behalf of, Tenzin Gyatso, the fourteenth Dalai Lama of Tibet. It was probably about three months or so ago that I felt the urge to take down from my bookshelf my copy of the book *The Path to Freedom* written by the Dalai Lama as his autobiography. And it was also then that I felt that another of my Spirit Guides had links with Tibet. I also felt that he was making his presence known in order to make a contribution to the book. The name that came to me was 'Raja Lampa'.

INTRODUCTION

Bob   Raja Lampa, are you ready and willing to introduce yourself to readers?

Raja   Yes, I am both ready and willing to do this.

As you know I was born in Tibet and grew up within the monastery to become a high Lama. I say 'high' Lama with the greatest humility because I know that this role entailed a great responsibility from me. However, I endeavoured to perform my tasks sincerely until it was no longer possible to do so under the new regime which entered into the 'Land of Snows'. In Spirit I continue to take my tasks seriously. These are to bring about a new understanding and a new recognition between peoples of different cultural backgrounds. I work with others to try to help people on Earth to find bridges of understanding, so that they can work together for the good of the whole.

This is a most pressing task at this time in World history and I try to play my small part in bringing this about.

When I lived in Tibet I was very concerned about religious differences which could cause conflict and unrest even though, on the whole, the country was unified under the Dalai Lama. Nonetheless, religion has to be seen as a means to come to God, and not as a goal for its own sake. It is a way, amongst other ways, of finding one's way to the Creator Being of the universe. So it is always a question, a need that is, of building bridges between people and cultures, so that true healing can take place. Perhaps this suffices as my introduction? **Raja.**

Bob   Thank you.

PIERRE

After my preoccupation with reading **The Path to Freedom** I felt my attention drawn in another direction. In my travels around the local charity shops I came across books to do with the Knights Templar. One of these was entitled **The Secret History of the Knights Templar**, a complete illustrated chronicle of the rise and fall of this Brotherhood, or Order. I noticed other volumes on the same theme to which I felt drawn. Now, without any further elaboration, I can just mention that I had been familiar with the Christian Impulse of the Templars for many years. This familiarity was in the context of my membership of the 'Camphill Community' and my work as a curative educator for some forty years until my retirement in 2012. As well as the outer work in living with and teaching children with special needs, the Camphill Community had also a more inner aspect which was to do with its spiritual and community-building impulses. These impulses were viewed in the widest possible context as helping to bring healing and harmony into our troubled World, so that 'the Good may come to Earth'. A 'Leading Thought' of the

Community contained a reference to the 'high ideal' of the Knights Templar. Namely, 'That in place of what brings quarrel and discord to men, there must come that which can bring the Good to Earth.' So, as I say, in this way I felt some link to these medieval Christian monk-warriors.

The name 'Pierre de Monfort' came to my mind and I again had the impression that a Spirit Guide wished to be included in my book. I will let Pierre now speak for himself.

INTRODUCTION

Bob   Are you ready and willing to introduce yourself to readers?

Pierre   Yes, I am both ready and willing to do so.

I was born in France and this is where I lived for all my adult life. As I grew up I got to know of the Knights Templar (The Knights of the Temple) and I felt at one with their aims and aspirations. I therefore joined their ranks as a man and I fought alongside my brothers-in-arms. However it was the inner commitment to the Christian ideals, to Christ, which really fired us in our earthly endeavours. When the Templars were exterminated in the 14th century I also met my own demise.

In Spirit I continue to stand for the ideals for which we died on Earth but I now see those ideals in the broadest way, to bring about salvation for humanity. I do not believe in violence but I do believe in the power of love to transform the earthly World. So, together with others, I do what I can to bring this love into human hearts and minds, through service to the impulse of Christ. The living Christ who is visible to all in Spirit who are open to his light and love. So this is my introduction to myself and my aims. God's Will be done on Earth. All blessings. **Pierre.**

Bob   Thank you.

*****

NB: Now, just to reiterate for the sake of complete transparency and inner freedom, I am recording 'the communications' which have come through to me. I am not asking anyone to simply believe them. Each person needs to make up his or her own mind about this or, perhaps even better, simply try to keep an 'open-mind'. This is what I also endeavour to do.

PAN

Since childhood I have always enjoyed to be walking outside in Nature. To be able to walk across open meadows, through woods, by the riverside, near the sea, etc. is, for me, a blessing. It helps to clear the mind and to see things in a better, freer perspective. I started jogging along the country lanes in the 1970s long before this activity had become a popular form of recreation. To be outside, in all weathers, was something I relished. Fortunately, in the various places where I've lived, there has always been easy access to the natural environment. So, in this respect, I certainly count my blessings.

Where I walk nowadays, part of the Cotswold Way in South Gloucestershire, I have a favourite old Oak tree that I lean my back against. I imagine that I then stand within the pure energy-field of this Ancient One, which I'm sure is quite literally true. I also make a point of thanking all the invisible beings who sustain and maintain the life of Nature, for what they do. Although I do not see them as such, I have no doubt in the real existence of this great variety of nature spirits and elemental beings.

It was perhaps six months or so ago that a friend of mine lent me a copy of a CD by R.Ogilvie Crombie (Roc for short) entitled ***Encounters with Pan and the Elemental Kingdom***. On this CD Roc describes quite candidly how he was actually able to see the, normally invisible, beings of Nature. This was not something that he had expected or at all anticipated, though all his life he had had a great love for the natural world. He also describes some of his meetings with the God or Lord of Nature, namely 'Pan'. I listened to this CD quite a number of times and on one of my walks wondered if perhaps Pan himself would also like to contribute to my book. When I asked this question, the reply was affirmative.

INTRODUCTION

Bob   Pan, can you introduce yourself to the readers of this book please?

Pan   Yes Bob I can and will do so.

I am known as Pan, the God of Nature and Lord of the elemental beings. It is my task to overview and direct the workings of Nature and the countless beings who are active within her, for the sake of humankind and the whole planet. Without a healthy, wholesome planet there can be no human life on Earth. Therefore my task is crucial for your very existence and it is my wish and endeavour to bring about real, conscious cooperation between Mankind and the Kingdoms of Nature. This cooperation depends on the right knowledge and on goodwill, God's Will.

My subjects in nature are willing to work with human beings but, to do so, human beings need to wake up to their true responsibilities. Above all to safeguard the life of Mother Earth they need to do all they can to ensure her wellbeing and good health. It is my task, and my hope, that this cooperation can come about and that many more people will participate in saving the Earth for Mankind and for the generations to come. All blessings, **Pan.**

Bob   Thank you.

NB: Whereas the previous contributors may all be described as regular Spirit Guides, Pan is obviously of a different spirit order, as also is Philip, who will introduce himself next. Nonetheless, all of them have in common the will and wish to be of help and support to us provided we, in freedom, ask for their help. The initiative lies with us, not them. In this sense we need to 'wake-up' to the reality in which we already live.

PHILIP

It was in February 2007, some ten years ago, that I went to visit a lady in her home. She told me that she was a medium, actually a 'trance medium'. The first thing she asked was whether I knew the name of my Angel. I said I didn't and she said that his name was 'Philip'. She also said that, 'He has wanted me to know this for a long time. When I need to ask for help, speak to Philip.'

Later that same day I turned to Joshua to ask if he had any comments about this visit to the medium. Amongst other things Joshua said,

> 'Yes your Angel, Philip, has been trying to get through to you for a long time Bob and he seized the opportunity which she presented to you this morning.'

I then went on to communicate directly with Philip. However I must admit my communicating with Philip has been quite sporadic in comparison to my speaking with Joshua and Dr John. Somehow, for me at least, it is a different sort of awareness to be mindful of my Guardian Angel, than of my other Spirit Guides. Though Philip did say, ten years ago,

'I am with you always as your higher guide and protector.'
So, I also, am still in the process of waking-up!

INTRODUCTION

Bob   So, finally, Philip will you introduce yourself to the readers?

Philip   Yes Bob, I will do so.

I am an Angel, a Guardian Angel to be specific, for Bob (Robert). I have been his Guardian Angel for all his incarnations and it is a task I am given by the Divine Godhead. In this I am one of the millions of guardian angels, nay billions, who take loving care of each human being who is assigned to them. Therefore, in this book, I represent the hierarchy of the Angels and can say that this hierarchy wishes to work in conscious cooperation with all human beings, in the same way that Pan and the Nature Spirits wish to work with you for the good of Mother Earth.

The time has come when angels and men and women should learn to recognise each other and collaborate to bring about a World of peace and harmony. These are not meant as empty words, but as a crucially important aim for all of us. Only thereby can God's Plan for humanity be realised. Only then can the fulfilment of the legacy of creation be realised on Earth and in Heaven. This is my task also, as part of the angelic hierarchy. God bless you, **Philip.**

Bob   Thank you.

So with all the 'Introductions' now completed we are ready to move on to the 'Teachings' which the Guides wish to bring through to us. Each Guide will take on one of the following chapters and each chapter will also include a 'Question and Answer' part. This allows a dialogue to take place in which, perhaps, some of the Teachings can also be challenged and tested?

Let me close by making the following remarks. As has been explained I met Dr John and Joshua Isaiah through Anne Lewis, the spiritual medium. Therefore Anne knew them, before I did consciously, and confirmed their reality. Another friend of mind, Neil, was a natural clairvoyant since early childhood. Since then he has developed his clairvoyant abilities consciously. Neil and I have often met for conversations about spiritual matters. On some of these occasions I have asked Neil to tune-in and see who I have with me in Spirit. Through doing this he has also seen Dr John and Joshua on either side of me in Spirit. Sometimes he has also observed a figure or column of light behind me. I rather assume that this is Philip.

When I had received communications from those Guides included in this book, I always made a point of checking with Joshua if I had received correctly? Joshua confirmed that I had done so every time that I asked. Nonetheless, the responsibility for sharing with you these Communications is mine. The title of this book, ***Trusting in Spirit – The Challenge*** remains, for me, an ongoing exercise and practice.

Addendum

It has always been my practice to seek for confirmations of my own spiritual experiences whenever possible. I see this as part and parcel of doing good research, rather than simply doubting myself! So near the end of February and in early March 2018 I had two sessions with my clairvoyant friend Neil. The purpose of these sessions was to invite all the Spirit Guides (including Pan and Philip) who contributed to this book to make themselves known to Neil's clairvoyant perception. These two 'Spirit-Research' sessions were extremely interesting. In the first of these all eight Guides appeared, eventually, though it was not altogether easy for Neil to tune in to some of them. It was rather like a first 'introductory' meeting. However, in the second session, two weeks later, we asked the Guides to initially come through in a way that was more familiar to Neil. This procedure worked very well and it was actually a very successful session. The eight Guides could be clearly identified through Neil's clairvoyant descriptions and my own knowledge of them. I had in fact already discussed my intentions for each of the sessions with Joshua prior to meeting with Neil and was assured of the Guides' cooperation with us. Near the end of the second session one of Neil's Guides, in Egyptian form, also joined us!

A third research session actually took place in mid-March. However the purpose this time was to put particular questions to the Guides, and thereby to come into a sort of running conversation with them. Neil asked the questions and I conveyed the answers as given by each of the Guides. Neil also described whatever he perceived clairvoyantly during this communication process. This provided for a very interesting session. Near the end, I invited Rudolf Steiner to join us. (This was something I had already in mind well before the session began.) I wanted to ask him if he approved of the work I was doing with the Guides, if he was agreeable with this? The answer, which Neil received, was 'Yes, absolutely', and Neil then had the impression of a very small child being cared for by a father. He also had the impression of Rudolf Steiner taking me by the hand and saying, 'Come on son'. This is something I can relate to, and feel very grateful for. It is my conviction that if we are drawn towards a particular spiritual teacher that we can then have an ongoing, spiritual, relationship and link with that teacher in freedom and love.

4

JOSHUA

TEACHINGS

Let me just point out that the following teachings from Joshua, together with the question and answer session which relates to these, is presented verbatim. I did not edit, or change in any way, what was received from Joshua. It reads exactly as it was given. The same forthrightness applies to the telepathic contents received from all the other Guides.

Bob So Joshua, I am ready to receive whatever you wish to say in this chapter of the book.

Joshua Shalom my friend, thank you for being willing to receive my words.

In the first place I want to point out to the readers of this book that I am a Spirit-being living in the fifth dimension of reality. This is where I live at present in a realm of Light and Love, and this is also where the other Guides who will contribute to this book also live. We live in this realm, this dimension of Being, but we have also lived in the third dimension of reality where you, the readers, live at present, ie. in your physical, bodily existence. So you understand that we, the Guides, have also experienced physical, bodily incarnation. We therefore know and appreciate what life is like on the earth-plane and what difficulties and challenges you face on this level of existence. This is precisely why we are keen to share with you information, knowledge, which can serve to lighten your load, to help you to cope with all that life brings towards you. Therefore it is with goodwill – with God's Will – that we are grateful to share with you, thanks to Bob our medium for this purpose, what will now be set forth. All blessings.

To begin with let me say that I lived a religious life in my former incarnation on Earth, I was a Jewish Rabbi. However, when we enter into Spirit and expand our awareness, we are not tied down to the beliefs or dogma which we held during our incarnation. We are much freer to appreciate, to experience, the richness and diversity of human thoughts and experience. It is a freeing from all that which narrows us in particular sects or divisions of human striving.

Now this state which we enter into when coming into Spirit realms is also a state which, more and more, should come about also on Earth. That is to say, a state of mind where 'live and let live' should be the motto of the day. A tolerance and ability to see that people from all walks of life and backgrounds, should be able to live out their own particular culture and beliefs while, at the same time, allowing others to do the same. There should therefore come about a new harmony amongst human beings – a harmony in diversity.

Now my friends we are not saying that this is always an easy thing to achieve. Indeed it is one of the great challenges of the times you live in, to foster such an ideal. And, believe me, ideals are far more important than you might imagine. Ideals maketh the man, or woman, as the case may be. By our ideals we fashion ourselves and the World we live in as co-creators with the spiritual substance which is needed to build a new future. So we would urge you dear friends to take seriously what you nurture as ideals in yourselves and in your children.

It is all too easy to simply go along with the flow, with the mainstream of life, without giving enough thought to what really matters. Examine yourselves and ask, 'What do I really want to do with my life?' or, not to make it sound too heavy and momentous, 'What do I want to do with this particular day in my life?' 'How do I want to live this day that it is worthy of who I truly am?' Can I, in fact, find a way of living, of relating both to myself and others, that satisfies my desire to be a person who is worthy to take his/her place in society, in the well-spring of human life on Earth?

Now this may sound all rather grand, especially when seen in the context of what I really have to get on with today in the nitty gritty affairs of life. Have I really got time to think deeply about my ideals, about the purpose of life, the deeper meaning of existence?

Maybe not, but we do need to realise that what we do today can make a difference, for good or ill, to the state of the World. Oh yes my friends, this is no exaggeration. The World will be different, have a different quality and ambience, if we take a different attitude to the part which we can play within it. You know that most of the news you hear on the television and through the media, newspapers, etc. is bad news. Rarely do the really important things which countless people do to improve the state of the planet hit the headlines. If you allow yourself to simply drink in, day by day, all the bad news, then it is hardly surprising that so many intelligent people feel depressed!

Depression comes about when hope becomes lost. Hope for a better future for ourselves and others, and this is a truly terrible state to be in. Nothing good comes of it. It saps the energy of life and makes us feel lost and afraid. It is a state that unfortunately affects more and more people in modern, technological society. What is the antidote for this? It is a new outlook which is based on a truly spiritual perception of ourselves and the World in which we live.

That is why I said earlier that a change in gear is now needed to lift humankind out of the heavy third dimension of existence into a higher and lighter frequency of Being. This is, I know, easier said than done, but it is doable! It starts with a change of thinking, with a willingness to look at ourselves and the World we live in with new eyes, to see things afresh and to pull ourselves out of the mire of day-to-day existence and day-to-day conditioning.

It is not simply in oppressive societies that freedom of thought is suppressed. Only we do not see it, we do not realise how much we are channelled into set ways of thought and behaviour that are restrictive to the human soul and spirit. The human being, as the crown of earthly creation, is above all a thinking Being. A Being capable of original and creative thought. When creativity is stifled then, instead, stagnation sets in and there is no way in which the full potential of a person can be realised. Only through a change of heart and a change in our attitude towards ourselves in particular can the wellsprings of creativity be uncovered. So this is what is needed in our times, in the times in which you live as human beings of the 21st century. It is a crucial time for unlocking your own potentials to do the good for the sake of all creation. And it is through an awareness of your Spirit Guides, for each of you has such Guides, that encouragement and help can be given towards fulfilling your true aims in life.

Each of you came to earth with such true aims. Aims and goals for this particular incarnation, this particular opportunity to help shape and fashion the World of which you are an essential part. Let no one be under any illusion that your particular contribution is any less than that of another. Each one of you has a real contribution to make in changing things for the better, in letting your own Light shine into the darkness of the World. Though the World is not really dark, it only appears so when viewed from a purely physical, materialistic perspective. Spiritually, the World is filled with light and love, a love which permeates every part of creation. It is this love which can light up your own life if you are prepared to receive it. You receive it as soon as you overcome the fearful thoughts and feelings which hold you back. Fear seems to be very powerful, but it is only as powerful as you allow it to be. It is like a balloon which, as soon as it is pierced, collapses into nothing of importance. The balloon of fear is blown up out of all proportion by the mindset that sees only the physical happenings in the World, that is unaware of the spiritual realities, which stand behind all existence.

And so my friends, we would urge you, in love and freedom, to break the balloon in which you live and see that things, all things, can then appear in a new light. A hope-filled light which speaks of a new Earth, in the sense of an Earth in which truly human ideals, tolerance, openness, love and kindness, rise to the forefront of our hearts and minds.

All blessings for this day. Shalom, **Joshua.**

QUESTIONS

Bob   Joshua, you refer to living in 'a realm of Love and Light'. This phrase 'Love and Light' has become rather a cliché which is used again and again, in, let's say, 'New Age' or spiritual literature. Can you say what this really means?

Joshua   Shalom my friend. Yes, I can say more about this. Both 'Love' and 'Light' are spiritual realities, actually substances you could say in the Spirit Worlds. They are not abstractions but inner realities of Being. Therefore, although it is true that it is a well-known phrase and, in that sense, could be seen as something of a platitude, to us who live in this fifth dimension of Being it is absolutely true to the reality of our existence.

Bob   You speak of the importance of having 'ideals' in life. Can you say more about this?

Joshua Ideals are substance in Spirit. Thoughts are substance in Spirit. Thoughts are not simply mental constructs as abstractions. No, in Spirit Worlds thoughts are the very fabric and structure of life. Therefore ideals, as refined and lofty thoughts, have a special part to play in fashioning the very fabric of the life and surroundings in which we live. This is already the case on Earth, in the third dimension of Being, only it may not be so obvious that this is not merely a subjective reality but also an objective one. Objective in the sense that very real structures are formed when ideals are living in a human soul and spirit. Worlds are built from the ideals which you nurture in your souls. So there is nothing abstract about ideals. They are the very substance of life itself in the Spirit realm.

Bob   You speak of the difference which each of us can play in changing the state of the World for the better. You speak about a change in our thinking, and of freedom of thought and creativity. Do you really think that a single person can make a shred of difference, really, to a World in which billions of people live?

Joshua Of course my friend, absolutely. The World is composed of individuals and what every individual thinks and does makes a difference to the whole. Do not underestimate the part, the role, which each of you can play. A single lit candle can lighten the darkness of a large room or hall. If one candle shines out then that room is not dark. Just imagine how much brighter it becomes if a hundred candles are shining out into that space. So, yes, what an individual does makes a difference and can also inspire others to do likewise.

Bob   But coming back to 'freedom of thought'. What do you mean by this?

Joshua   Freedom of thought my friend is essential if you are to break out of the prison of fixed viewpoints and heavy dogma. I say 'heavy' dogma because such entrenched viewpoints really do bog you down and put a weight around your neck, so to speak. In order to move up to the fifth dimension of Being, it is necessary that a new lightness of Being can come about. Dead, fixed thoughts are a weight that restricts you. Free thoughts, that is to say thoughts which can embrace and work with other thoughts, bring about a new unity and lightness of Being. They do not imprison you but set you free in your thinking beings. So this is why it is so important to break free of all that restricts and narrows your outlook.

Bob   You say that the World, our World, is already filled with 'light and love'. Well this is difficult to believe isn't it when there are umpteen conflicts and wars around the globe at any one time.

Joshua   Yes you are correct to say that there are many conflicts, but do not let the conflicts blind you to the spiritual realities and the true humanity which more and more emerges out of this chaos. The great danger my friend is that people are blinded and conditioned to see and hear the worst. This is the danger of the daily diet of bad news.

Yes, there are awful things happening, we do not deny that, but in spite of this there is a tremendous force for good that is also working behind the scenes. If more and more people learn to recognise and acknowledge the good that takes place, then the whole World becomes lifted up into a new dimension of Being.

So do not think that all is lost and is doom and gloom. This is not the reality, but the cloud which is pulled down over many peoples' vision by the mindset that breeds fear and insecurity. Remember great spiritual Beings are helping you – all of you – to raise your vibrations and your perceptions to higher and lighter levels of Being. Love is the greatest force in your World, and ours, not fear. Fear only appears so when the forces of darkness are given free rein to blinker your vision.

Bob   What do you mean by 'forces of darkness', isn't this a bit dramatic?

Joshua   No, not really. There are beings who aim to deflect you off course from your true spiritual aims and goals. They are there to test your resolve and determination, but also to strengthen you through their very adversity to your real goals in life. Everything has a purpose, even the obstacles and so-called dangers which you need to face. So my friend, take heart, much is happening at this time to help human beings find their true Selves, their Spirit-Selves, which lie at the core of who they really are.

Bob   Some people will say that all this talk about 'Spirit' is really eyewash! It just doesn't carry any real conviction to the reality of life on Earth.

Joshua   Well, what you call reality can be far from the truth. The truth needs uncovering from the layers of ignorance and confusion which prevent a person's truth to be known to themselves. This is the aim of all really spiritual work, to uncover the truth. 'The truth will set you free' is a saying which is indeed true, but which also needs to be experienced by each person.

47

Bob   How can we allow more love and light into our hearts and souls? What is the key to this?

Joshua The key my friend is to be who you truly are. You are truly a being of love and light, but you do not yet realise this. Too many coverings of fear, of conditioning, of dogma, prevent your own light and love being recognised by yourselves. Release the bonds which keep you imprisoned in your own restrictions, your own chains, and let what is actually in you fly forth.

We, as Guides, can help you towards this realisation when you request our help. We are there precisely for that purpose. Know of our reality, trust in our sincerity to assist you in every way we can, and then we work together for the good of the World. All blessings, **Joshua.**

Bob   Thank you.

5

DR JOHN

TEACHINGS

Bob   So John, I am sat down pen in hand and ready to write what you give me. Are you ready for this?

John   Yes Bob, I am ready.

What I want to say this morning comes of course from my perspective as a doctor, a healer. That was my profession in my last earthly incarnation and it is an impulse which has remained with me in the Spirit World. Therefore I want to look at things through this prism, to see things from the point of view of how we can maintain good health, rather than from, 'How are we to cure our illnesses?' Prevention is much better than cure!

To begin with it is important that people adopt a healthy lifestyle. Whatever you may do in terms of your work or profession, it is essential that you spend time and energy in maintaining optimal health. Now I am not saying that this will always be easy for people to do given the stressful and busy, if not frantic, lives that many people have, but nonetheless this is where we need to begin.

Even quite simple measures can prove effective, very effective even, provided they are adhered to on a regular basis. We do not need to spend a fortune buying special foods and vitamins, nor getting all manner of equipment, to stay healthy and strong. No, it is quite sufficient if people simply adopt sensible and cost-effective strategies in their lives. What do I mean? I mean, for example, walking places instead of jumping into the car. Walking is one of the best forms of exercise we can do. Why do you think we have legs if it is not to use them to get us from A to B? In the past people used to walk a great deal because there were often no other means of transport. Now however we have become lazy and happily rely on driving ourselves for even quite short distances that we could easily manage to walk, if we allowed ourselves a little more time. So, my friend, this is the first point I want to make in our book. Walking not talking is the answer to a good deal of our health needs.

Now what else can we do? Again keeping things simple and well within our capacity to fulfil, I would include breathing. To learn to breathe healthily. What do I mean by this? I mean to sometimes fill our lungs to capacity instead of indulging in habitually shallow breathing. Especially when out in the countryside, surrounded by all that is growing naturally, a good lungful of air can do us the world of good. We take in the air, the breath of life, and with it we take in oxygen as a life-giving force and energy. We breathe out the carbon dioxide, the poisonous air, which our friends in the plant kingdom can take in to build their own bodies. It is a natural interchange between us, as humans, with the plant kingdom.

In this we see the wonderful love and harmony that is at work in the World. Could anything be so simple as learning to breathe fully? Thereby receiving into ourselves the energies we need to maintain a healthy body.

Yes, what else can we do to help ourselves and I do mean it literally, to help ourselves? We do not always need other people to bail us out of situations when, with a little bit of effort, we can work our own miracles. My friend, in addition to walking and breathing we have, of course, eating. It is most important that we eat healthy, nutritious food. This may sound trite, but it is true that many people happily fill their stomachs with rubbish! I am sorry to put it as plainly as this, but it happens to be the truth. You would not put water into your car's tank and expect it to perform well! Neither can you expect to maintain good health if you continually feed yourself with processed food that contains chemical additives, colourings, preservatives, etc. It simply doesn't work. Fresh food in the form of vegetables, fruit and other naturally grown substances will give your body the vitality and energy it needs to perform its functions to the full. I know what I am saying here sounds obvious, and I am not putting forward any earth-shattering new ideas or theories, but nonetheless these things are essential to maintain good health. And it is good health I'm interested in, health of body, mind and spirit. We cannot expect to have or maintain good health if we indulge in faulty habits and ignore the basic needs of our physical instrument, ie. the physical, material body.

I think you and our readers will agree that what I have said so far is not 'rocket-science'. It is commonsense but, unfortunately, there is a dire shortage of commonsense nowadays, especially in a technological, fast-moving society. People who still live in more natural surroundings, indigenous, so-called simple people, often have much more commonsense than us modern technocrats! I say 'us', for though I am living in the Spirit World, I nonetheless see and understand something of the modern conditions of the 21st century.

I am after all a human being who, for a time, am living in a different dimension but who nonetheless is deeply concerned about the state of my fellow human beings living in the third dimension, incarnated in physical, material bodies. This is why I do the work that I do in trying to help people, from Spirit, on the earthly plane of existence. This is also why I am so grateful when I and my team in Spirit find suitable and willing channels to work with on Earth, ie. 'spiritual healers' in particular.

In spiritual healing we do the healing from our side of life and send the required energies, the healing energies, through those who work with us. It is a subtle, yet effective, way of helping to bring about harmony and balance in people who need our healing help. We do not claim that we can cure every ill under the Sun, this would be ideal perhaps but, for good reasons, this ideal is not always possible to manifest. People get ill for all manner of reasons, sometimes for their own greater good. Illness can teach necessary lessons on a person's path of destiny, the path they themselves have chosen to walk along even before they were physically born on Earth. So in some cases it is not always possible to effect a physical healing, even though we will always try our very best to help in every way possible. We also have to recognise the choices that people have made out of their own greater wisdom and the lessons which need to be learnt in this particular lifetime.

Anyway, having said this, let me continue to mention a few more ways in which people can optimise their health, and do everything they can to lead a healthy, wholesome lifestyle. Obviously things, or rather habits, such as smoking, drinking alcohol, drug usage and indulging in obsessive and unhealthy activities should be avoided at all costs. We know that some people are drawn towards activities such as these, as a form of compensation for other difficulties they encounter in their lives. Unfortunately, however, this is not really a solution but, instead, compounds the very difficulties they seek to overcome. It only makes matters worse, not better. Therefore we encourage you to avoid these pitfalls if at all possible and it is always possible to avoid them because you, as individuals, do have free-will. You have options and choices to make. Your choices determine your lives. You are not driven by compulsive forces unless of course you are already in an ill state of mind or body. Our whole thrust is to help you find ways, simple ways, to maintain good health of mind, body and spirit. The three are closely connected, they are not separate entities but form part of your whole Being. Whilst you live in a body, that body needs the right sort of nourishment. When you leave that body behind at death you will receive a different kind of nourishment. But whether within, or without, a physical body, love is the most essential nourishment for all human beings. I am not being sentimental about this, but factual. No human being can survive intact without sufficient love.

So I would urge you, my friends, to foster love – unselfish love – to the greatest extent you can. It is something you need for day-to-day living and it is something which can be given freely without limits. I speak of course of true, real love. Not of that which is referred to as 'love', but is nothing more than self-gratification and emotional indulgence.

Love in its true form is the substance that sustains all life in your world and ours. It is the connecting thread, the means by which all life is maintained and flourishes. So with this thought in mind I will now end my own contribution to our book. All blessings, **John.**

Bob   John, you have put emphasis on 'walking' in a healthy lifestyle. But, unfortunately, some people with disabilities cannot walk!

John   Bob, my friend, thank you for pointing this out. Yes, I mean walking as a good example of taking regular physical exercise and I certainly do not wish to cause any offence to those people who are restricted in their movements through disabilities of any sort. All blessings.

QUESTIONS

Bob So John, are you ready to answer the questions I want to put this morning after I've read what you said before?

John Bob my friend, yes I am ready and waiting and will answer your questions to the best of my ability.

Bob John, you say that you were a doctor in your last life on Earth and that you carry on with this healing impulse in the Spirit World. Is this really possible to do? I mean, to continue as it were in one's profession after death?

John Bob my friend, yes it is possible provided that this has been an impulse which really was carried in one's heart, so to speak. It needs to be an impulse which deeply drives one to want to continue to serve in the same way. To be of service to one's fellow human beings. Obviously if a person had a profession which was not really something that inspired them as a vocation, as a 'calling' in life, but was much more 'a job', then it would not be carried beyond death in the same way as a true vocation is.

Bob John, you emphasised the need to lead a lifestyle that helps maintain good health and you included 'walking' as a good form of exercise. However, as I mentioned after your talk, not everyone is able to walk. So was your point really focused on regular physical exercise per se?

John Yes my friend, it was. Thank you for pointing out that not everyone is able to walk, for whatever reasons there may be. Physical disabilities, accidents, other impairments, etc. Yes my friend, I really wanted to emphasise forms of physical exercise that enable us to keep the body in good form, so to speak. Now this exercise can take different forms and it can be geared to the needs and possibilities of each person. People are different and there is no one answer that fits all.

However, my point is really that exercise is important and this is something which nowadays, even in childhood, can be neglected. Therefore problems, health problems, such as obesity for example, are modern problems in advanced societies. 'Advanced' meaning where people do not need to exert themselves physically in the way that indigenous people do in rural and agricultural societies for example.

Bob   You talk about 'breathing' John, that is deep breathing as opposed to habitual shallow breathing. This reminds me of the recommendation which Harry Edwards, the well-known English spiritual healer, advocated for people to breathe deeply. I think he called it 'characterised breathing'. So do you mean the same as he did?

John   Yes my friend, very much so. Harry Edwards was well aware of the importance of exercising the lungs and of taking in to oneself the life-giving oxygen. He knew that this was a ready source of life and energy and, for this reason, to practise this simple strategy to improve their health.

Bob   John, as a third element you also refer to good food and to having a healthy, nutritious diet. Can you say more about this because it so often features in 'health warnings' and in people putting forward all manner of advice about what we should or shouldn't eat?

John   Bob my friend, again I would have to say that diet, like exercise, is a very specific thing for each person. Because people are constituted individually it is really a matter of seeing clearly what works for the particular individual.

Now, having said that, one can of course give more general advice, such as eating fresh foods rather than processed foods. Of course this makes sense. However, in a sense each person needs to find out what their body needs to maintain good health. There needs to be a feeling, a sense, for what agrees with you or not. Of course with children it is necessary to guide them along the right lines. Parents have a big responsibility to guide their children to eat healthily, rather than to simply indulge their whims and fancies. Though, the truth be told, young children do have an inbuilt sense, a body-sense, for what is healthy for them or not. If parents do not spoil this sense by giving them the inappropriate foodstuffs, then children will more or less know what is good for them. So, especially in the case of children, to avoid spoiling their taste is a key strategy for maintaining good health and good eating habits.

Bob   John, when you talk about 'spiritual healing' and sending through energies from Spirit to help people overcome illnesses, you also mention an important point. Namely that 'people get ill for all manner of reasons, sometimes for their own greater good'. Can you say more about this since it is a concept which many people would probably find quite bizarre. After all we modern people see illness as a 'pain in the neck', so to speak, to get rid of as soon as we can.

John   Yes my friend, I see exactly what you mean and, yes, this is very much the modern, scientific view of illness and disease. However this view completely leaves out any understanding of 'karma', to use the Indian term, and reincarnation. These considerations are however central to a deeper understanding of why one person gets ill and another doesn't, and yet are both living in similar physical circumstances. You see it really does come down to the needs of each individual, each person. And these needs go beyond birth and death. These needs have to do with their eternal spirit-being, and the pathway that their soul is taking to arrive at the realisation of who they truly are. This pathway is planned for by their own true Being in Spirit but, once incarnated, and wrapped up in a heavy material body, the person does not normally carry any knowledge of their own pre-ordained plan. This plan may well include the need to experience a particular disease, illness, or so-called accident. These events will then take place in order that certain lessons can be learnt and further progress made on that individual's path through life. A path that is designed to help them arrive at a new recognition of who they truly are.

So my friend, you see that life is complicated and it is not always easy to unravel what particular lessons need to be learnt beforehand. It shows itself in the course of going through the actual experiences. Of course we, as healers, will do all we can to ease the way and to cooperate with the person's higher Self, and therefore we can give no guarantees of cure or 'success' in any particular case. We simply do all that we can to help.

Bob   John, you refer to certain habits that we should 'avoid at all costs', such as smoking, drinking alcohol, drug usage, etc. But could there sometimes be good reasons for actually following such habits? I mean, for that particular person? For example, I've heard that for certain 'spiritual' persons smoking helps to keep them grounded!

John   Well my friend, there is something in what you say. There may be individual reasons which justify a certain dependence, shall I say, on one or the other substance. However, as a general rule, such dependence is to be avoided. We get into tricky waters when we start to justify this or that practice by reference to one or another individual's need. It is fraught with dangers and, therefore, I remain with the advice I have already given.

Bob   What about the over-use of electronic devices such as mobile phones, which is so typical of modern life nowadays? How is that regarding health?

John   Bob my friend, mobile phones are a scourge in some ways because they continually radiate the person with electromagnetic radiations that are detrimental to good health. So it would be wise, to say the least, to limit the use of these devices to a minimum. Of course most people, including many doctors, are unaware of the adverse health effects of these electronic things but, nonetheless, they are not good for physical or indeed for mental health. We are aware that this could be a very controversial point because people are so much in love with their phones! However it is an area where much research needs to be done, to see what effects these things have on the health of the whole person.

Bob   Finally John, you refer to the power of love as a real power in our lives. A power for health and strength you could say?

John   Indeed that is so. It is the very stuff of life, the staff of life. Without love everything becomes barren and dead. Life can only thrive when love is active and, without this activity, life deteriorates into nothing. Yes, literally, nothing. However, on the other hand, nothing can exist unless love brings it about. Love is the source of all life-forms both on planet Earth and in the Cosmos as a whole. Therefore it is a force, a power, which needs to live more and more strongly in human hearts and souls. All blessings, **John.**

Bob   Thank you.

6

MARKOS

TEACHINGS

Bob   Markos, are you ready to work with me and bring through teaching in this chapter?

Markos   Yes my friend, I am ready and waiting. Let us start.

Bob, in my last incarnation I was born in Greece. I became a teacher there and I was known for my philosophy. I am not saying that I was one of the great philosophers of Ancient Greece, I make no such claims, but nonetheless I did have a certain following of those who were interested in my thoughts and beliefs. Now however I live in Spirit and my thinking has moved on, shall I say, from the particular notions that I entertained in my earth-life. I can now see things, see events and beings, with greater clarity and therefore I am able to put my previous thinking into a wider, broader perspective.

Now my friend, let me come to the point. I wish to make a contribution to the book which may be of help and assistance to those readers who are seeking for greater clarity and certainty. Especially those readers who are more inclined, shall I say, to thinking deeply about the problems and challenges which life presents to them. What I want to say and share is as follows.

Life presents us with many riddles. Riddles about our own personal existence, but also riddles about the World at large. Sometimes these riddles appear insuperable, as if we are left with feelings of bewilderment and uncertainty as to whether we will ever be able to make sense of all these problems. I say 'problems' in the sense that there are questions, big questions, which need answers. And answers are often not to be found easily. Sometimes it may take years of struggle before we are able to see meaning and sense in what has presented itself to us, both inwardly and outwardly.

We feel as if our search for answers is sometimes abortive, as if no light can be shed on what appear to us to be important questions for life itself. However my friends, this is not really the case. It is all a matter of where we turn to receive enlightenment for the answers we seek.

Above all, we should seek for this enlightenment not from books or other material sources, but from the depths of our own heart. It is in the heart, our own heart, that we shall succeed in finding the answers to the most important pressing questions of our life. The heart, our heart, is the source of true Wisdom. Most people do not know how to listen to the answers which lie in our own heart. By 'heart' I do not mean of course simply the physical organ which science believes is like a pump, pumping the blood around our body. Yes, it is truly a centre for circulation, but in a far more profound way than is normally imagined. The heart circulates love, and love is not simply an emotion but is a living substance. It is this living substance of love which unites all life on the planet, and also beyond the planet. Love is that which circulates through all life-forms and especially those life-forms which have sentience and consciousness. Consciousness exists on all manner of different levels my friend. I do not limit myself to speaking simply of human consciousness and awareness. No, what I mean by consciousness exists throughout the universe, the wider Cosmos, and is not restricted to the life known on planet Earth. The whole universe teems with consciousness and with life. We in Spirit find it amusing, if I may so express myself, when your scientists of today grope and search for any signs of life beyond the confines of planet Earth. They search, of course, with the means available to them as scientists based on physical and logical means of exploration. There is of course nothing wrong with this, but it is restrictive and narrow compared with those means of exploration which take into account the spiritual and psychic dimensions of life. If more scientists would become open to such extended possibilities, then they would be amazed at what there is to be discovered in the further reaches of the Cosmos. The universe in reality teems with life, but it is not in the form which is known in a materialistic sense. There are echelons of Beings who have no physical, material bodies but are nonetheless as real, more real in fact, than the physical entities which science so far is willing to recognise.

I understand my friends that to some of you, all that I have said so far will sound simply the stuff of science fiction. A fiction which has no sense in reality. Well, though I understand that is how it may sound to you, nonetheless it is the truth. The truth is often stranger than fiction! Now, returning to where we began, namely 'How can we answer the perplexing and pressing questions which life presents us with?' I should like to say the following.

I have intimated to you that answers to these questions can be found within, when we turn to the wellsprings of wisdom in our own hearts and souls. This is not idle talk. This in fact points us, you, in the direction that must be trodden if you are really serious about solving the problems which beset your paths. The heart, spiritually, is an inexhaustible source of knowledge and wisdom, but how to turn to, or tune into, this source is the key question. It is like finding the key that can unlock the door, behind which lies the answers to the questions that you seek. This key, my friends, is found in prayer and meditation.

Now you may say 'Oh yes, we have heard a great deal about prayer and meditation, but can we really believe that this is anything other than pure subjective experiencing, which has no grounds in objective reality?' Well, my friends, you first need to experience for yourselves what prayer and meditation can do for you, before arriving at any final judgements. Don't put the cart before the horse! I mean, don't judge what is possible before you have practised and gained your own experience of the subject. Only by making your own experiences will you be in a position to really know what you are talking about. 'Oh yes,' you say, 'but what is prayer and meditation that we hear so much about nowadays from different sources?' If we look at religion, I mean conventional religious groupings, then we may feel that all their prayers, mumbled ceaselessly perhaps, do not amount to much in reality. They seem to have limited, or even no power, to change anything concretely for the better. The World continues with its seeming disasters in spite of all the prayers offered up by the faithful. Yes my friends, I fully understand your viewpoint. However, do you really know what effect real prayer has? And by 'real prayer' I mean prayer that is divorced from selfishness and self-seeking behaviours. Prayer that is truly offered for the good of Humankind, and not for selfish ends. Such prayer, true prayer, can move mountains. Mountains of doubt and despair. It is therefore a question of learning to pray, to relate ourselves to the Beings of Higher Worlds, of the Heavens if you like, in such a way that they can respond to us to effect real change. This can be done, but it does require some real effort. We do not say that it is easy, but it **is** doable.

With regards to meditation which has been a discipline long practised in the Eastern religions, this has a more inward direction than prayer. Both prayer and meditation build the bridges from the physical to the Spirit Worlds, but meditation has a more inward and personal character.

Not everyone will feel drawn towards a more meditative way of life. In some ways it is more challenging than prayer, but it is no less effective in establishing a rapport, a dialogue, between us in Spirit and you in the body. And it is this dialogue, this rapport, which is so important if you really wish to solve your own and the World's problems.

Behind all material happenings there lie spiritual forces and beings. Nothing is simply as it seems to your physical senses, and you can only come into touch with these realities when you train your heart and mind to perceive differently. When you do this the World takes on new meanings for you, as does your own life.

So, my friends, I would urge you, encourage you, to seek the answers to your problems, challenges, concerns, on a prayerful and meditative path of learning. This path leads you to the depths of your own hearts, and in your hearts lies the wisdom and the love which will unlock your own hidden resources. These resources will give you the strength and courage to meet all that life presents you with, and give you the means to change and deal with it accordingly. This is what I wanted to say in my contribution to this book. All blessings, **Markos.**

QUESTIONS

Bob   Markos, are you able, willing, to communicate with me this morning?

Markos   My friend, I am both willing and able to do so and look forward to our session.

Bob Markos, I came to know of you through the psychic artist Peter John and I have the portrait of you which he did for me in my room. May I first clarify if you were actually born and living in Greece in your previous life? Peter John told me you were Greek, but with Byzantine connections.

Markos Bob, my friend, yes my origins were Greek and whilst I spent some time in Greece growing up, in my profession as a merchant I moved to other places outside Greece itself. Therefore what Peter John has told you is correct, and I do not claim to have been domiciled in my birth country as an adult. Still, being Greek it was very much that spirit and way of thinking that lived in me.

Bob Markos, you say that since you live now in Spirit you are able to put your previous, earthly thinking into 'a wider, broader perspective'. Is this typical for those who live in Spirit or is it particular for you?

Markos Bob, my friend, this is very typical when we make the transition into Spirit. Our life is seen as it were from 'above', in the sense that we can survey it from a distance, so to speak. We are not so tightly bound-up with who we were when living in the body. Therefore our thinking, which was very much influenced by our upbringing, social context, etc. is also no longer tied into that particular mode of operation. We can see, or start to see, things, events, people, from a different, broader viewpoint. It is a liberating experience we could say, since it enables us to be more flexible and fluent with our thoughts.

Bob Markos, you refer to many riddles and problems which life confronts us with, and you say that answers to these can be found in the human heart. Can you clarify this assertion please?

Markos   Yes I can. The heart is the well-spring of life and love. It has hidden depths which are unknown to ordinary medical science even though, physically, its functioning is acknowledged and its structure appreciated. However this is the physical, material heart. You have also a spiritual heart organ, an organ for perceiving your destiny and enabling you to be in touch with your own true Self, call it the higher Self if you will. It is this aspect, this higher dimension of the heart that I am pointing to. If a person learns how to listen to his/her heart in the right way, then a well of wisdom is uncovered and this can inform of those matters which press upon them. Matters which cannot be solved simply by logical thought or ordinary reasoning. This is why it is so important to wake-up to the hidden, inner dimension, of one's heart, as the centre of one's organism.

Bob   Alright, but how do we listen to, or get in touch with, this inner spiritual aspect of the heart?

Markos   Through prayer and meditation. Through learning to live in the silence and listening to what wants to speak to you when you have real, pressing questions in your life. They need to be real questions, important questions at that moment in your life. Not just trivial things which have no great significance for yourself or others. When you have a real question, learn to go inward and put this question to the core of your own Being. Then listen, quietly, and see what answers start to emerge for you.

Bob   Markos, in putting the questions as I am, I ask them by reading through what you have previously given as 'teachings', but not reading the teachings all in one go, but bit by bit.

I can see, having now read all you said before, that you put emphasis on prayer and meditation as the means by which to make the connection to the heart's wisdom. Markos there are many prayers and many meditations and many meditation techniques available nowadays. How does a person choose what is best, right, for them?

Markos   My friend, that is a good question because, as you say, we are spoiled for choice nowadays. But it is also true what you say in as much as each person, each individual, needs to find what speaks to them. Here your Guides can be helpful if you ask them to guide you along the right, or best track, shall we say. Your Guides are there to help you. They have been especially chosen to be of particular help to particular people, and they therefore know what can most help at any particular time. Think of them as advisors if you will, perhaps counsellors, who have your best interests at heart. When you feel you need guidance to find the right direction to go in, turn to your Guides and ask for their assistance. They will do all they can to help, whilst respecting your free will and your own choices in life.

Bob   But many people may see so-called 'Guides' as nothing more than a figment of imagination. Wishful thinking, instead of solving your own problems yourself!

Markos   Yes, they could be viewed in such a way, which is a pity since they are nonetheless there and keen to be of service.

Bob   Could you say a bit more about the life of the universe? You claim that it 'teems with life'.

Markos   Indeed it does, and on all manner of levels and dimensions. It is a total illusion to believe that life only exists on the physically observable level. No, it exists on physical and spiritual levels of being, and it is possible to get to know other life-forms through inner development and acquisition of new organs of perception. When these organs are developed, whole new worlds of life and being become known. The World is as you perceive it, but it is also limited by the extent and degree of your ability to see, perceive, what is actually there. Seeing is believing, but believing is not always seeing things as they actually are!

Bob   Markos is there anything else which you would like to add before we close today?

Markos   My friend, I think we have covered the most important points. I would only add that I am most grateful to be able to make my contribution to this book, which we hope will prove of benefit to many readers. All blessings, **Markos.**

7

RED CLOUD

TEACHINGS

Bob   Red Cloud, I am ready to write, are you ready to give me your teachings?

Red Cloud Yes my friend, I am ready. Let us start.

My friends, in my last incarnation on Earth I was a member of the Sioux tribe of Indians living in North America. My name is Red Cloud and in that last incarnation I was a chief of the Sioux people. Now, like other Guides who are coming through for this book I live in Spirit Worlds. I would like to bring to you the following teachings.

You are spirit-beings clothed in human form. You, each of you, have come to Earth for a specific purpose, nothing is arbitrary. Each of you has a mission to fulfil in this earth-life and it is the task of your Spirit Guides and your Angel to help you to fulfil your chosen mission. This mission, for each of you, was something that you decided upon well before you were born and it is something that then determined where you were born and to whom you were born. Nothing is left to chance, all is prepared carefully in order to achieve the aims which you have set yourselves. I emphasize that you yourselves have set the aims and goals of your own lives. You have decided, out of your greater Wisdom, exactly what it is you need to develop yourselves and to make a step forward on your journey home.

What do I mean by 'your journey home'? What am I referring to? I am referring to the task which all human souls are engaged upon, whether they realise this or not in their conscious minds. All of you are intent to find your way back to the eternal

Godhead – 'the Great Spirit' in the language of my former people. This is a long journey which takes many lifetimes to enact. It is often a perilous and difficult journey and is not for faint-hearted souls. Courage is needed and determination to carry on when obstacles and hindrances are placed along your path. Nonetheless it is a glorious journey I would say, because it leads step by step to the goal of attaining your own God-hood. 'God-hood', what do I mean by that? I mean that inwardly you are already a spirit-being. A spirit-being clothed in a body of flesh and blood. But although you are a spirit-being, you are still on an evolutionary path of development. This means you are on the way to developing your true, human potential. This potential is a glorious thing to behold.

We, in Spirit, are better able to see your potential than you are when you are encased in a heavy material body. This potential, which is really what you are in reality, is at a point which reflects the stage of the journey which you are on. Each person, each individual, stands at a different place on that journey. It is your task, your chosen task, to complete that journey bit by bit, stage by stage, so that your full potential can shine out like a new born star. The universe needs your Star, and without that star shining forth into the darkness of space, the universe is not yet complete.

You may think, dear friends, that I am simply being romantic, taken up by fancies and thoughts which have little bearing on day-to-day realities of life. No, my friends, you are wrong, because in your innermost being you know that your task is to be a member of the Light World – the World of Spirit Beings. In order to achieve this task, lessons have to be learnt. These are the lessons which you have prepared for yourself in Spirit before you were born on Earth. You yourselves fashioned these lessons, you yourselves decided what needed to be learnt in your current earthly lifetime.

Now, my friends, you may say, 'But I have no memory of any such tasks or lessons, so how can it be that I planned these if I have no recollection of them?' Yes, my friends, you are right that you do not normally, or usually, have any clear recollections of what you yourselves have planned and prepared whilst in Spirit realms. Nonetheless the truth of the matter is that in your deepest being, in your own heart, all is contained and can be revealed to you step-by-step. How can it be revealed to you? By life itself of course, since you are the one that is experiencing what life brings towards you each day. You are the one who has to deal with all the challenges, the ups and downs, the obstacles and hardships which befall you. And in these very hardships you learn important lessons. Whether these hardships take the form of illnesses or accidents or other blows of fate, it is you yourselves, my dear ones, who have determined the causes that bring these events into your lives. Only you, no-one else, is responsible for the lessons you have given yourselves.

Do not waste your time and energy in blaming others for the difficulties you encounter. You are the architects and builders of your own destinies. You have done this out of your greater wisdom. You have done this because you know exactly what is needed if you are to progress along your chosen pathway. No-one else determines your fate but you yourself. This, my friends, is a powerful thought and I would ask you to take it seriously. Give it serious consideration and then see how, living with this thought, affects the way you look at events that enter into your life. You will find my friends that these thoughts are a source of strength to you, because you begin to realise that nothing is there by chance. Everything has meaning and purpose in your own individual life.

My friends, I think I have nearly said all that I need to for today. I realise that what I have said may raise many questions in your minds. For some of you, you may feel more confused now than you did when you started to read this chapter. It may feel as if your whole world has been turned upside down. 'How am I expected to deal with all this?' you may say. 'Before now I always felt that it was others who were shaping and determining my path in life, giving me opportunities or blocking my path. Now you tell me that it is I myself who am the driving force in my own destiny. This is difficult to take in and accept.'

Yes, my friends, it may be difficult for you to accept at once, but may I suggest that you live with what I have said here and see, gradually, how that rings for you? Rings in your own heart. In your heart you have all the answers to your own questions. I am merely pointing the way, giving you a helping hand so to speak. Your own Spirit, your own true Being, is the best Guide you will ever have in your life. We, as Spirit Guides, are simply helpers for you. Because we are in Spirit Worlds we can see more clearly than you often can, just how you are progressing on your paths of life. But it is you yourselves who are walking these paths. As the Indians, my brothers, used to say, 'Only if you step into another man's shoes and walk his walk, will you truly know how he feels.'

We, in Spirit, can to a limited extent step into your shoes, to the extent that you allow us to do so. We will never impose ourselves on you, we respect your free will and the choices you make for yourselves. But we are there, here, to help, and if you call upon us we will do all we can to throw light upon your path. With these words my friends, I leave you in peace and send my love and greetings to you all. My blessings, **Red Cloud.**

QUESTIONS

Bob   Red Cloud, are you ready and willing to communicate with me now?

Red Cloud   'How' my friend, yes I am both ready and willing. Shall we start?

Bob   Red Cloud, you say that we ourselves have set the mission and aims of our earth-life well before we were born. How can we test that this is true?

Red Cloud   Bob, my friend, you test it by life itself. If you actively take up this thought my friend, say as a hypothesis, and then on that basis look and see how your life unfolds, then, I dare say, you will see how things fall into place. True, it may not at first be obvious to you why this or that blow of fate befell you. You may feel that this was unfortunate or unfair or just bad luck. But, on closer reflection, and seeing how one thing leads to another, you may then perceive that there is actually a higher wisdom at work which is guiding you along your life's path. This wisdom comes from your own true Self.

Yes, it is a wisdom also supported by others, by other Spirit beings but, essentially, it is you yourself who have decided which way your life should unfold. So my friends, if you allow yourselves the possibility that what I have said is true, and then test that truth by life itself, you will find the confirmation which you seek.

Bob   Red Cloud you speak of 'your journey home' as finding our way back to the eternal Godhead – the Great Spirit. How, many modern secular people might ask, can we really understand this notion of some eternal Godhead? Some great or supreme Spirit?

Red Cloud My friends, we understand that for many of you the thought of a supreme God, some all-knowing, all-powerful Being seems like science fiction or just sheer fantasy. Nonetheless, this is actually the reality of the universe in which you live. There exist many beings, Spirit-beings that is, of different degrees of development, of different ranks you could say, in the structure of the World – the World-All. But there is one Being above all, and that is the Being that has brought this universe into being. Now this may be a difficult concept for some people to get their heads around, but in their hearts they actually already know of this truth. The problem, or challenge, is how to enter into this knowledge of the heart when the head and its particular, especially scientific, way of thinking has grown so strong in your modern culture? In other more natural cultures such as I lived in in my previous life, there was no difficulty for us to accept the 'Great Spirit' that presided over the whole universe. This was something that was actually a part of our experience, because we could perceive with our hearts and not only our heads. So a new sort of perception is needed for modern people to grasp the truth of the Godhead – the head of the Gods, so to speak. In your own hearts this new perception can be found, but it does require a 'change of heart', a change from a purely materialistic culture to a spiritualised culture.

This is not the same as religion in any dogmatic sense, but rather a way of looking at the World such that what is really there can speak to you. The World-Word sounds out in your own hearts and souls.

Bob   When you say that, 'the universe needs your Star', referring to our true potential as a Spirit-being to shine out, isn't this all rather poetic and romantic?

Red Cloud   Well my friend, it may appear so but, in fact, I do mean it also quite literally. Each person becomes like a star that shines with his/her own light. You radiate light out into the universe when you realise who you truly are. This is something which we in Spirit can perceive. It is not something theoretical or abstract, but a fact of our experience. You are in a real sense all 'star children', children of the Universal-All.

Bob   Red Cloud, you say that we ourselves are the architects of our own lives. That we have determined the lessons which we need to learn. Now this may sound plausible in, shall I say, normal circumstances, but some people have very difficult lives to lead. Some people suffer abuse as children, others are born or grow up in war-torn countries, or experience famine or drought. Can we really imagine that anyone, in their right mind, would choose such a difficult destiny?

Red Cloud   My friend, we understand what you are saying and we do not pretend that these very difficult circumstances are easy to accept as anything we ourselves, you, would have chosen freely. Nonetheless, it is not for nothing that such difficult and painful conditions need to be endured. It is easier to see this if one can see what this experience has meant for such a person, where it has led them, and how it has shaped their own beliefs and resolves.

Bob Red Cloud, I must interrupt you there because, for example, in the case of child abuse it can happen, I think, that in some cases the child grows up to become an abuser precisely because of these early negative experiences. How can this be positive in any way?

Red Cloud My friend, you are right that these things are difficult to understand when you see them close up. It is only when you can see them from a higher perspective that you perceive and realise that a greater lesson was present for that individual, or even for that particular group of individuals. There is always something positive to be gleaned from even the most difficult and devastating circumstances, but this cannot easily be seen from the 'worms-eye' point of view. It needs an overview to really separate the wheat from the chaff. Still, we do accept that these are difficult issues for anyone to take on board who has to suffer, from their own higher choice, such problems in life.

Bob Red Cloud, you say that, 'Your own true Being is the best Guide you will ever have in your life.' But this begs the question, 'How can we, the ordinary person say, discover or find their own true Being?' How on earth can we do this?

Red Cloud You do this my friend by creating moments of quiet within you, and then listening. Listening for what can start to speak in the silence. This was something that the Red Indians knew about when they had to deal with the great problems in their lives. They knew that in the stillness – like the stillness of the mountain lake – they could hear the voice of the Great Spirit, and this voice reflected their own true Self, their very Being.

So we could say, learn to enter into the stillness and learn to listen carefully to what reveals itself to you there. This revelation comes from your Being, the one who you truly are. All blessings, **Red Cloud.**

Bob   Thank you Red Cloud.

8

RAJA LAMPA

TEACHINGS

Bob   So, the Guide I know as Raja Lampa, are you willing and ready to communicate with me, or not?

Raja   Yes, I am willing and ready and looking forward to make my contribution.

I am a Tibetan Lama, or at least I was in my previous life on Earth. In Spirit I no longer hold this office, or rank shall I say, but am a spirit with other spirits. Here we form a community of spirits who work together for the sake and the good of the World. In this I find my meaning and purpose in life. So I thank you my friend for allowing me now to make a contribution to this book in which, as Spirit Guides, we share out thoughts, beliefs and experiences, our knowledge, with those still in the body.

Let me say this to begin with. I have known what it is to suffer on Earth. I have known what cruelties can be inflicted from one human being to another, and how people can mistreat and abuse others for the sake of power and greed. These things I had to experience in my last life on Earth and they shaped the love that I now feel for all humanity. I know that only the power of love can truly transform and transcend the darkness and fear, which are engendered by those who wish to exert their influence on others in an abusive or coercive way. Of course people can exert influence on others also in a good and health-giving way. This is the other side of the coin, so to speak.

However, there is much greed and egotism to be found in earthly life, and this therefore requires a concerted effort on behalf of those who are determined to do all they can to improve the World for the sake of all sentient beings. Let me say the following my friend. I am happy to contribute to this book for the reason that I recognise that what is written therein will succeed in touching the minds and hearts of some of those who will read it. Perhaps not everyone will be touched in the same way or to the same degree but, nonetheless, the book will convey to those who are ready to receive its message and teaching, that there is a Spirit World which is ready to help you. Is ready to give you strength and courage to stand your ground in face of adversity and hardship. This Spirit World works for the good of all humanity and does not shirk from giving its forces to help bring about the best that is in humanity.

There is in fact much good to be found provided only that one searches in the depths of the human soul and spirit. People have great resources of goodness in them because they are, at heart, truly Spirit Beings, clothed in the bodies of earthly human beings. This was something that I was already very aware of in my last incarnation on Earth because the religion which I followed and the training I received prepared me to recognise the spirit in each person. Yes, even in those who would persecute us. It is just a question of searching in the depths, and not being blinded by the outer, passing appearances. Spirit lies deep within each human soul, just as the pearl lies embedded in the oyster and grows there stage by stage, until it is discovered by prising open the shell.

We, my friend, need to learn how to open up the shell, the hard shell, that surrounds the jewel within, the essential Spirit Self. In order to do this we need to occupy ourselves with spiritual thoughts and spiritual knowledge and wisdom. Then these thoughts stir our feelings to life, and we become sensitive to the deeper realities of life. No longer just satisfied with what lies on the surface of the lake, so to speak, but rather we plunge into the depths to discover what lies within. It is a revelation to see what riches are to be found in each human soul when the outer appearances are laid aside. We then discover that the Spirit is no mere abstraction, no mere concoction of the human mind or imagination, but an actual reality of Being. This reality of Being was what the Buddha pointed to thousands of years ago. He discovered the eternal kernel within his own soul, and he knew that this kernel lived also within each person. His teachings were aimed at helping each person discover their own Self, their Spirit Self.

Now my friend, you may wonder why am I speaking about all this. What relevance can it possibly have in a modern, secular world? Well, my friend, that is just the point. Unless human beings start to wake up to their own true reality of Being, they will continue to walk along in a thick fog. They will be unable to discover their true aims and goals in life and, subsequently, many people can then be sucked into all manner of unhealthy and unwholesome lifestyles. All these are really a sort of compensation for what they are missing in life. They have lost their essential meaning and purpose, the very reason for which they altogether incarnated into a human body. If this purpose gets lost then their life becomes meaningless, becomes shallow, and bereft from purpose and intent. Intent that is, to fulfil their life's mission which they set themselves before making the great descent from Spirit Worlds. Therefore my friend, we must do everything we can to help and encourage human beings to align themselves with their Selves. That is, their true Spirit Selves that stand behind their outer lives on Earth.

To make this connection, to forge this link, is the whole purpose of meditation and contemplation. By sinking into the stillness, into the silence, the human being starts to become sensitive to their own guidance, their own inspiration. They find within, what they have lost outwardly. This is what I wanted to share with you today. This is what I wanted to contribute to your/our book, because unless this knowledge, this self-revelation, becomes known and experienced by each human soul, life will be a perpetual mystery. More than a mystery, it will be an aimless chaos! A seething cauldron of impulses and drives that have no sense or order. And that is really a grave danger of the times in which you live my friend. Namely, that people are driven by their drives and instincts in a self-centred and egotistic way. Instead of working for the greater good of all, rather a selfish determination to satisfy themselves irrespective of the needs of others. I am sorry to paint such a gloomy picture but you see it is essential that a waking-up to the true kernel of humanity comes about in your time. Otherwise there can be a slide into darkness.

We, as Spirit Guides, are willing to do all we can to be of help and encouragement to you all, but the initiative has to come from your side of life. We are not allowed to interfere in your free will. However, as soon as a request is made to us, we can act. We receive permission to intervene in a helpful way. So this is the message that I wish to leave you with today. Ask for help and we will help in every way we can. Your asking opens the door for us to enter into your lives. 'Ask and you will receive' is the word to be found in the Christian teaching. It is a teaching that has been known through the ages. If you follow it, then a great cooperation can take place between us in Spirit and you in the body. All blessings, **Raja Lampa.**

Bob   Thank you.

QUESTIONS

Bob   Raja Lampa, are you ready and willing to answer questions to do with your teachings, or not?

Raja   Yes, my friend, I am ready and willing to do so. I will try to answer your questions to the best of my ability.

Bob   You speak about the resources of goodness within each human being. This reminds me of how St Francis of Assisi recognised the good in each person. However, we have seen, and still do see, great cruelties perpetrated by some people. Indeed some of the atrocities done by human beings against other human beings are beyond belief. Yet they have been done. So how can we really accept that every person has, 'great resources of goodness in them'?

Raja   My friend, what you say is true. Great evil has been done on Earth in the name of 'liberation', 'cleansing', 'freedom', etc. in the most twisted and corrupt ways possible. All this has happened and no doubt, to some extent, continues to happen. People are persecuted for their beliefs, for their religion and faith, or for the colour of their skin and racial descent. All such crimes against humanity are to be abhorred.

Yet it would be a mistake to think that because these evil deeds are done, that there is no hope left for redemption and salvation. The force of good, the power of love, is far greater than all the evil combined. The power of forgiveness can work wonders and help to awaken conscience in a human soul that has become dulled and lethargic through abuse and indoctrination. So yes, while I accept all that you say, I still know that spiritually, at the core of a person, any person, there is an infinite source of love and goodness.

Bob　　Whilst what you say sounds truly altruistic and admirable, nonetheless I still find this difficult to accept given the atrocities which are committed against others, including women and children. Aren't some people really beyond redemption?

Raja　　No, they are not. Not even the worst of the worst is beyond redemption, through the power of love and forgiveness. I do not say this is easy, but it is certainly possible. Love remains to be the most powerful force in the universe and if this force is tapped into and cultivated then nothing, absolutely nothing, can stand against it.

Bob　　Is Christ, or Buddha, the source of this cosmic, universal love?

Raja　　Both are my friend. Both Christ and Buddha practised this love for all humanity. Both teach that forgiveness, compassion and love are the forces which will overcome all adversity and redeem all inhumanity.

Bob　　You emphasise the need for people to align themselves with their true Spirit Selves, in order also to follow their goals and aims in this life. But many people would say that this Spirit Self is really just wishful thinking, or rather perhaps, just an illusion. It's not something real, is it?

Raja　　It is indeed real, more real than you might imagine, because it is who we really are. The outer appearances of life are illusionary, if they are not illumined by a knowledge of the Spirit that lives in all things and beings. It is Spirit that is at the core of all life, not matter. So to wake up to our true Selves is not just a luxury, it is a necessity if we are to fulfil our tasks and missions on planet Earth.

Bob   You speak about going within ourselves, of entering the silence, in order 'to become sensitive to their own guidance, their own inspiration.' How do we know that this works?

Raja   You know that it works if you do it and make your own experiences. No one else can do it for you, only you yourselves. Deep within each human being lies their own fount, or well, of wisdom. It is there, but it needs tapping into. If a person loses themselves in all manner of outer distractions, then they will never find that eternal core of their own being. It has to be found within yourself. 'The Kingdom of Heaven is within you', is a Christian teaching and it is true. But to come to know it, practise going deep within yourselves.

Bob   But some people might say that's just another form of escapism, like putting your head into the sand!

Raja   Yes my friend, they might say that, but it is only when you do it and make your own experiences, are you then in a position to judge its truth or falsity. So we would advise you to do it, learn to meditate, learn to sit in the silence, and see how this practice enriches your own life.

Bob   Finally, you speak about a cooperation between us on Earth and Guides in Spirit. Why?

Raja   Because, through this cooperation, we can achieve much more, also in a shorter time, than if we remain apart and isolated. Working with your Guides will enable you to make greater progress in your own development and this, in turn, will help the development of the whole World.

What you do for yourselves spiritually benefits all sentient beings. It is a service done for all humanity and for the planet as a whole. All blessings, **Raja Lampa.**

Bob   Thank you.

9

PIERRE

TEACHINGS

Bob   Joshua, is Pierre ready to communicate with me, or not?

Joshua   Shalom my friend. Yes he is, and he is looking forward to this.

Bob   So Pierre, please tell me what you want me to write.

Pierre   Thank you my friend. I realise that you do not know me as you do Joshua, since he is one of your main Guides. Nonetheless, I have made a link with you and wish to make a contribution to the book.

I was born in France in my last incarnation on Earth and when I grew up I was associated with that stream of history which is bound up with the mission of the Knights Templar. It is a stream which is known to you to some extent from your 'Camphill' days is it not? At any event I aligned myself to their inner striving and to the ideals which they nurtured in their hearts and souls. Now, like the other Guides, I live in Spirit Worlds and it is from there that I seek to be helpful to my fellowmen (or women) as I did when I lived on Earth. I would like to give you some teaching today which can form part of your book. It is this.

Life on Earth has many trials to endure, it is not an easy option. I experienced certain of these trials in my last incarnation. Nonetheless it is important that we realise that all trials have also a higher purpose in our lives. We ourselves set such trials in order to learn certain lessons and to progress spiritually. Nothing is for nothing, so to speak. Everything has something to teach us and thereby to enable us to grow stronger and more awake to our own situation in life. I mean by this that it is necessary for us to go through trials and difficulties in order to make progress in a spiritual sense, even when in a physical sense there seems to be no why nor wherefore for our tribulations.

Now I am aware that what I have said so far is very much repeating what the other Guides have also said. There is however a purpose in repeating certain important things. It gives them confirmation and validity, as it were, from another independent source. We know my friend that you are aware of how research is done, especially in a qualitative sort of way, when dealing with human issues and circumstances. We cannot give 'hard' evidence in the same sense that physical scientists often aim for, but by confirming certain facts from different viewpoints and perspectives, we try to lend weight to what we wish to share with you. So repetition does have sense and purpose behind it. Now my friend, let me continue to enlighten you if I can about other important matters concerning the higher realities of life.

You come to Earth to learn lessons but you also come to help transform the whole planet. Many people today are concerned about the health and wellbeing of the planet, as indeed they need to be. The planet suffers in various ways and when I say suffers I mean it. The planet, Mother Earth, is a living being. She suffers when human beings suffer and there is much happening at the present time which causes much grief and sorrow. I am sorry to bring such things to your awareness in as much as there seems to be such a lot of 'bad news' around as it is. However it is necessary to face the facts and, by doing so, to perceive more clearly what needs to be done. In order to bring healing and harmony to Mother Earth, a fundamental change in attitude is needed by human beings. I mean especially, modern, technologically-minded, human beings. There are still some indigenous, simple-minded peoples who have a natural wisdom and feeling for how the planet needs to be treated with respect, reverence, and awe. But, unfortunately, this is not the case with the great majority of modern people. They are too busy making their own lives work, than devoting much care and consideration to the planet as such. Of course there are exceptions to this, such as 'Friends of the Earth', but not everyone is active in this sense.

No, a much wider awareness needs to be developed if real healing forces are to be made available for the planet and all its many life-forms. This needs a new sense of responsibility, a new feeling that the Earth, Mother Earth, is a most precious resource, is literally, the ground under our feet. This ground can only be strong and firm if the soul of the planet, the Being of the Earth, is also acknowledged and respected rightfully. Now you may wonder where all this is leading. Well, it leads to me asking all human beings to take into consideration the part that they play, individually, in nurturing and caring for the planet as a whole. It is not enough to expect someone else to do it. Each person needs to feel involved and active. Then, and only then, will there be a sufficient number of dedicated, seriously minded, individuals willing to make a real effort to save the planet and to preserve its life-forces for the good of all. When this really happens then the future of the planet will be preserved for generations to come. And the generations to come need this planet, Mother Earth, on which to incarnate and fulfil their destinies.

You cannot fulfil your destiny if you have no ground to stand on. This ground can only be available for future generations if the present generation takes pains to care for Mother Earth, with a real sense of responsibility and love. Love for Nature, love for all that the Earth provides, love for the blessings which the Earth daily gives us.

This will strengthen peoples resolve to do all they can to love the planet, that is to love the soul and spirit, the Being, of the planet. The planet is no dead object. It is a vibrant, light-filled, sphere of humanity that exists for the very purpose of providing the place where destinies can unfold and be fulfilled. It would surely be madness to undercut the very ground under our feet. It would surely be madness to jeopardise the future of our children and grandchildren and great-grandchildren. So I pray that this new sense of responsibility and love for Mother Earth will arise in many, many people. This is what I especially wanted to say today. All blessings, **Pierre.**

Bob   Thank you.

QUESTIONS

Bob   Pierre, are you ready to work with me and to answer questions regarding your teachings?

Pierre   Yes my friend, I am both ready and willing to make my contribution to your/our book.

Bob   Pierre, you say that while you were on Earth in your last incarnation you sought to be helpful to your fellow men and women. Can you say more about this please?

Pierre   Yes my friend. As I have already told you, I was born and lived in France in the 13th/14th centuries at the time when the Knights Templar came to prominence. As a young man I was filled with the ideals which these Knights bore within their hearts. These ideals were centred around restoring, or rather bringing about, the Kingdom of Heaven upon Earth. By this I mean that the Knights felt that the power of the Christ, the love of the Christ, should be brought right down into daily life and affairs. Their goal was to manifest Christ's love and power upon Earth. It was a high ideal that they set themselves, and it was an ideal that reverberated also within my own heart and soul. Therefore I tried to live this ideal out in my daily life and to be of help and service to others as best I could. This is what I meant by saying that I wanted to be of service and help to my fellow men and women. It was an ideal of the Knights Templar to which I also felt aligned.

Bob   Pierre, you speak of undergoing trials in life, difficulties, which help us to become stronger and progress spiritually. While this sounds very plausible, many people may feel this is a rather romantic ideal of the hardships people go through, particularly when these hardships were not of their own making. For example, the terror attacks which take place, seemingly at random, and inflict death or injury upon others. How can we understand or make sense of such seemingly senseless, indiscriminate acts of aggression and hatred?

Pierre   My friend, what you say is true. Many things occur in life which seem a senseless waste of life and limb. Mindless acts of terror you could say. Yet from a higher viewpoint even these things can have sense and meaning. I do not mean in terms of any form of justification, but rather in terms of bearing positive fruit for those who suffer them.

Bob   Pierre, can I stop you there please, because what you have just said may well seem nonsense to many people!

Pierre   Yes my friend, I know that it can appear like that. Nonetheless you must realise that the consequences of such actions is not simply what it appears to be when viewed on the purely material level. The human being is more than body and flesh and blood. We are Spirit-beings clothed in flesh and blood. Our higher Being sees things from a very different angle than our ordinary personality. Yes, great pain, suffering and hardship can be, is, experienced on the ordinary level of being, but our higher Self sees things from a different perspective. Remember we have all gone through numerous traumatic and severe circumstances in the course of our various incarnations. It is not for the first time that we meet violence and danger.

Bob   Pierre, even though I can accept that there may have been difficult, even life-threatening circumstances in our previous lives, nonetheless in the modern context these events are still very shocking, especially if you're caught up in it yourself.

Pierre   Yes, this is of course true. In no way do I wish to underplay the trauma and grief that can be caused by murderous acts of violence. Far from it. Nonetheless there is a higher viewpoint which sees such things in a context not limited to the everyday and which can see that, even out of such terrible circumstances something positive will come. Lessons will be learnt that enable people, on all sides, to make steps in their own development.

Bob   Pierre, turning now to what you 'especially wanted to say', namely, learning to care for the planet as a whole. Just this week a blow was put to this aim by the USA deciding to withdraw from the Paris accord on curbing CO_2 emissions, to help restrict worldwide climate change. What do you think of this set back?

Pierre   Yes, it is a set back as you say. It is short-sighted to hold a view which does not see the World as a whole. The planet is the home for all humanity and for the many other life-forms that exist in that reality of being. Therefore it does need a concerted, a unified, effort to change things for the better. This is what I mean when I say that it is short-sighted to make decisions which set the World backwards rather than forwards.

Bob   Any further suggestions, advice, as to how to move forwards?

Pierre   Yes my friend, my advice would be to help all human beings to wake up to the realities which lie behind the outer appearances. There is a spiritual reality of being behind everything that is material and physical. There are spiritual beings who are active in trying to maintain the health and well-being of the planet. To learn to cooperate with these beings is what is needed. Concepts need to change. It is not just a matter of seeing the World as a solid, physical, object – a ball of matter in space revolving around the Sun. No, it is necessary to come to see the Earth as a living entity, a Being in herself, and many other beings are working hard to support her life-systems. To work together with these beings would be a huge step forward for humanity, but of course this is a step which only those who have spiritual insights can aspire to.

Bob   So what of the rest of us?

Pierre   Well, the rest must do all the practical things which they can, seen on the material level, to sustain the planet and, above all, to counteract the pollution and decimation of the planet's natural regenerative and life-giving forces.

Bob   Pierre, I suggest on this positive note we will stop for today?

Pierre   Yes my friend, let us indeed stop for today with positive and constructive thoughts in mind. God Bless, **Pierre.**

The immense importance of Pierre's warnings about the need to care for our unique planet should be obvious to any thinking person today. Actions are called for if the pollution and damage already endured by Mother Earth is to be repaired and, ideally, reversed. This environmental theme is now taken up with real heartfelt passion by Pan, the god of Nature.

10

PAN

TEACHINGS

Bob Joshua, I will make the attempt again to channel through teachings given from Spirit. I want to turn to Pan to see if he wishes to contribute. Will this work?

Joshua Shalom my friend. Yes it will work. Simply be a clear channel and let Pan come through as he wishes.

Bob Right Pan, over to you.

Pan My friend, thank you for allowing me to speak through you. Yes, I am indeed Pan, Lord of the Elemental Kingdom of Nature and overseer of the workings of Nature upon Mother Earth.

It is my task to see that there is harmony between the Kingdoms of Nature so that the right balance is maintained between the different forms of life on the planet. This is no easy task, particularly when the human kingdom is so set upon taking from the Earth, from Mother Earth, a living Being, but is not similarly prepared to give to the Earth what she needs. It is a very one-sided affair and it does not bring about any healthy balance. Rather than balance, a very large increase in the negative energies and forces comes about, because human beings are so often driven by greed and egotism.

What can be done about that? Knowledge is needed, real knowledge of the disastrous effects of this sort of selfish behaviour. Why do you think that earthquakes occur, for example? Why do you think that forest fires can go unchecked and run havoc over a landscape, destroying homes and properties in its wake? Why do you think that the Earth is depleted and impoverished in large areas? All this, and much more, has come about, is coming about, because of Man's misuse of his abilities and his blatant disregard of the needs of Mother Earth. Something needs to change, and soon, if the Earth, the Being of the Earth, is to recover the strength to sustain an ever-growing human population. Do not imagine that there is an inexhaustible supply of foodstuffs available on the Earth. The Earth can only provide for human needs if humans for their part treat the Earth with respect, reverence and humility. Humility is really in short supply nowadays. Human beings are too full of their own importance and do not realise what a risky game they are playing when they disregard the needs of the planet which is their Cosmic home. Their Cosmic home at least, whilst they live in physical, material bodies.

How, I say again, can we help human beings to wake up to their responsibilities and gain true knowledge and understanding of what they are doing? This is really a huge problem and one which cannot be solved by me alone! No, a cooperation is required. A coming together of human beings with those invisible beings, invisible to them that is, who work tirelessly at maintaining Nature in all her manifold forms. Behind all material phenomena is Spirit. Spirit works to bring the physical into manifestation. But 'Spirit' is not an abstraction. It is composed of countless beings, and these beings each have specific tasks to perform in the husbandry of Nature. There are beings that take care of the soil, those that flow in the water, those that breathe in the air, those that bring the warmth and fire element. These 'elemental beings', which have been known to some humans under a variety of names, are really there. They, together with a whole host of 'nature spirits', from fairies and elves to gnomes and salamanders, from pixies to leprechauns, to undines and sylphs, all these maintain the fabric and substance of the natural World.

Only if there comes about a living cooperation between these beings, my subjects, and human beings can Mother Earth thrive and be healthy. Failing this cooperation there will be one natural disaster after another. These disasters can be avoided, they are not inevitable. Each disaster is a 'wake-up call', a desperate call from Mother Earth to knock some sense into peoples' heads and, more importantly, into their hearts. Knowledge is needed, and once knowledge of the real state of affairs is gained, and acted upon, then real change for the better will ensue. Yes, the World needs to be transformed, but what it will be transformed into depends on human beings in the first place. Human beings are the custodians of the Earth, of the planet which is their dwelling place in the Cosmos. If they learn to respect the planet, love the planet and learn how to make bonds with all those nature spirits and elemental beings who work to sustain the life of Nature, then a real transformation for the better will ensue. Without this however, much tragedy will come to pass and great hardships will be inevitable.

The choice is yours. We are willing to work with you to cooperate in service to the World-All, but you need to play your human part.

So my friends, let me encourage you to wake up to the realities in which you now live as if in a deep sleep. Start to work with us, even though you cannot see us with your physical eyes. Nonetheless, know of our existence. Know that the Divine Being has put you on the planet to bring about a great transformation of both yourselves and the planet. Your destiny is one with the Earth and that is why the Lord of Life, the Cosmic Christ, has also united his Being with yourselves and your planet. Let His love, which is also the power of Life, stream through you and then the planet, Mother Earth that is, will also be filled with new life. To bring this new life into existence, through you, is the task which is meant to be, is, yours. Only, you need to do it! Only when it is done is it truly effective. This is what I wanted to say this morning. All blessings, **Pan**, Lord of Nature.

Bob   Joshua, did I receive these words aright or not so?

Joshua   Shalom my friend, yes you did. You were overlighted by Pan when you received these words.

QUESTIONS

Bob   Pan, are you ready and willing to answer the questions I will ask?

Pan   Yes my friend, I am both ready and willing to do so to the best of my limited ability.

Bob   Why do you say, limited ability?

Pan   Because I am not omniscient, I am not God but merely a servant of God and therefore I also have my limitations.

Bob   Pan, you speak of the Earth, Mother Earth, as 'a living Being'. What do you mean by this?

Pan   I mean by this that the Earth, the planet on which you live and have your being is, in fact, a Spirit Being in her own right. A Spirit Being who is recognised and acknowledged by other Spirit Beings in the Cosmos.

Bob   What do you mean by such a planetary Spirit Being? How can we understand this?

Pan Whether you can understand this as a modern human being is of course a big question. Unfortunately the perception of the Earth as a planet is much influenced, nay determined, by the very materialistic outlook which modern people, particularly most scientists, have of the planet. They see it as a conglomeration of dead substances, of chemical elements if you will, which are not imbued with life, but dead and devoid of life. Nothing could be further from the truth. The planet is filled with life and being on all levels, both above and below. It is a living Being in exactly the same sense that you are. The planet, Mother Earth, has a soul and spirit part, as well as a physical body. Therefore it is nonsense to think of the Earth planet as some object spinning in space and travelling around the Sun. It is not an object but a living, breathing Being.

Bob This description might well be the stuff of mythologies but hardly of hard science!

Pan Precisely, and that is the problem, because until there is a fundamental re-think of the nature of the planet on which you live, there will not be the will or insight to do justice to the true needs of the planet, ie. to Mother Earth.

Bob So how do you suggest we can do this?

Pan By taking on board the spiritual perspective. By taking account of the real Being of Mother Earth, by learning to communicate with her through your feelings and intuitions, instead of just using her as some object for your own gratification.

Bob   How do we learn to communicate with the Earth, with the Being of the Earth?

Pan   You can only do this when you approach her with reverence and humility. You cannot force your way into her favour, so to speak, you need to approach with humility and ask for what you need.

Bob   Should we not rather ask her what she needs of us, than ask for what we need?

Pan   You are right of course in this. However, it is a two-way process. By asking for what you need, you also give Mother Earth the opportunity to express her needs as well. The two work together, it is not a one-sided affair.

Bob   Pan, I'm still not clear how we go about this communicating. Can you elaborate on this, make it clearer?

Pan   Yes I can. You should start where you are. See what are the local needs of both yourselves and your environment. See how you can improve matters in all manner of different ways. Caring for your environment, picking up litter for example, thinking what you use and what you throw away, etc. In quite, or very, practical ways seeing how you can care for and appreciate your natural environment. This is an important form of communication with Mother Earth. What you do locally affects the whole, the whole planet.

Bob   Can we turn now specifically to the realm, or work, of the 'elemental beings'. The beings who work to sustain and encourage the whole life of Nature. How can people become aware of their reality and of their work?

Pan   By opening themselves towards the wonder and blessings of Nature. By noticing all that grows and has being and life around them in their environment. If there is gratitude and enthusiasm for the blessings of the natural world, then the beings that work within it are attracted to such human beings. Instead of being repelled, they draw closer to people and can even make themselves known to some of them who are sufficiently sensitive.

Bob   But do you think that human beings would take greater care of Nature if they knew that all manner of elemental beings and nature spirits are working in it? Would it really make any difference?

Pan   Possibly not if it is viewed as some sort of abstraction or of some fanciful play of nature, an entertainment if you will, which is unimportant for the real business of life. However, if the work of these beings is taken seriously, if it is taken as essential to maintaining the health and wellbeing of Nature, of Mother Earth, then a real cooperation, a real symbiosis, between humans and elementals is possible. This could be, would be, enormously fruitful and helpful. It would show clearly in the results which would follow.

Bob   Do you mean, for example, what happened at the Findhorn Garden project in Scotland?

Pan   Yes, that is a good example which was intended to set a prototype for many other such projects in cooperation between the elementals and human beings.

Bob   But has it had the desired effect? Did it have enough influence, let's say on the mainstream of agriculture, horticulture, and the like?

Pan   No it didn't unfortunately. Instead we see that greed and money making have had far more influence on the husbandry of the Earth, and these are the wrong motives. Service to the Earth needs to replace self-service and exploitation of Nature's resources.

Bob   It does seem to me that one way or another husbandry of the Earth, of the whole planet, is a huge problem. Is it really solvable?

Pan   It can be if there is enough goodwill on the part of human beings, and especially if they ask us for help in the right spirit, with the right motivations at heart. Then it will be seen how miracles, so to speak, can come about in the realm of Nature. So it is really up to you, to you human beings, to have the will to make a positive change. If you work with us, then solutions will be found to questions of nurture and nourishment for the whole planet.

Bob   Well Pan, given major questions and issues such as climate change, pollution, environmental degradation, impoverishment of the soil, etc. etc. there is a huge amount to be done.

Pan   Yes there is, but if each person would start to become aware of the needs of the environment, your environment, and do something about it, then the bigger problems would also become manageable.

Bob   Pan, I think we should draw to a close. But one last question is about your reference to the 'Cosmic Christ' and the Earth. How can the Cosmic Christ help us to solve our problems and also help the Earth?

Pan   He does this through His love. His love can transform the whole planet, can nourish the whole Earth and humanity, if it takes root in human hearts. This love, if it lived in your political leaders for example, would change the way they think and the sort of policies they would put forward. To align oneself with the Cosmic Christ is to allow love to rule the World, instead of power and force. Love transforms, it does not rule with power and force. This would create a very different sort of World than you live in at present. Love and blessings, **Pan.**

Bob   Thank you.

11

PHILIP

TEACHINGS

Bob   Philip, my Guardian Angel, are you ready to communicate through me now, or not?

Philip   Yes my friend and brother, I am ready to communicate through you. Thank you for inviting me to do so.

Bob, my brother in Spirit, I am indeed your Guardian Angel and as such I have accompanied you on your earthly path over all your incarnations. It is my task to watch over you and to help you stay true to your own spirit goals and aims. In other words, my friend and brother, it is my task to guide you to your true destiny in each earthly life. This is something that I do joyfully and also with a sense of deep responsibility. It is no light task for a Guardian Angel to watch over and guide rightly his/her earthly companion. It is in fact a profound responsibility to do this task. Why, you may wonder, does every person, every human being, have his/her Guardian Angel? Well it is of course for the reasons I have already said in reference to you my friend, but it is also that I myself may progress in my own evolution.

All beings are on a path of evolution, of development and progression. What do I mean by progression? Well, think of life as a school, a school in which we learn and progress through our lessons. We each have particular lessons to learn, and only by doing so can we make the necessary progress to move from stage to stage in our education. If you like, to move up through the school to higher grades. So it is also for me and for all other Guardian Angels. We need opportunities to learn and progress just as you do. Now we are not saying that it is exactly the same for angels as it is for humans. Those progressing in the sphere of human evolution are on a particular evolutionary pathway. This pathway leads through repeated incarnations on Mother Earth, the planet which is your learning ground.

With angels things are different, in that our pathway is through serving the needs of those in our care. We live a life of service, a service that has been ordained to us from the Divine Source of all life, God if you will, or better said, the Godhead. We, as angels, do not incarnate into physical matter as you do. We do not need that sort of material, physical experience. We rather live in the World Ether substance and have our being in this finer realm. We are grateful for the service we are able to give to the human beings under our care, under our 'wings' you could say allegorically. It is a joy to us when we see a person fulfil their own chosen destiny, because we then know that they have learnt the lessons which they have set themselves before they were born on Earth.

All of you set your own lessons. We only accompany you, we do not determine what you should learn in any particular life. That is not our task. It is your own higher wisdom, your Spirit-Self, which directs you to learn this or that in your life. Of course, when you are born into matter you no longer retain a memory, or knowledge, of what your higher Self has set before you as goals to attain or to strive for. We have that memory however, and therefore it is our task to help you keep to your own resolves. This is not always easy! You can be distracted and pulled into all different directions by circumstances that come towards you. We also cannot force you to keep to your own resolves, your pre-natal resolves.

We respect your freedom of choice and cannot interfere with your decisions. However, if you ask us for guidance then we are permitted to do just that. We will do this by giving you signs of one sort or another, to help you to see which way to go and how to proceed in the way that you yourself have determined beforehand. We can do no more than 'ring some bells' for you to follow, so to speak. Whether you then listen to these bells is again up to you. When you do listen, we have good reason to be joyful and happy for you. When however you do not listen, or see what is set before you, then we have cause for sorrow and heartache. Yes we are very dependent in our feelings for how things go with each of you that is placed in our care by the Divine Source of Life.

Well my friend and brother, what else can I tell you that would be important for those who read your book? To be honest there is not that much more to tell, because I have already told you the essence of what we angelic beings do for you. Of course there are many, many angels. Millions, billions of us as in your reckoning, just as there are billions of human beings on the planet at any one time. But, it is your own Guardian Angel that is special for each one of you. We have been chosen for our task by Beings of higher wisdom than ourselves. There are many ranks of such beings in your universe. The whole universe teems with life and consciousness. It is a complete illusion to imagine that you live in a 'dead' universe, simply filled with stars and galaxies. No, life itself abounds in myriad, diverse forms. There are beings who live on the other planets of your Solar System, but who do not require the same conditions as you do on Earth. 'In my Father's house are many mansions' is a saying that you know from Christian teachings and it is indeed a true saying. But these 'mansions' are rather levels and states of consciousness, than actual places in any physical sense. States of consciousness to which particular beings gravitate, so to speak, because this is the level that they have reached in their own evolution and development. The universe is full of life and this life is expressed through many different levels of consciousness. And yet there is also a One-ness to be found. Beings are not separate in your physical, bodily sense. They interpenetrate and form a complete one-ness or wholeness. That is why communication is possible between all different levels of Being. There is a vibration which runs through the different levels, uniting all beings of whatever rank they may be.

You are just as connected to the highest level of being as you are to me. You can call on the highest levels of being, as you can call on me to assist you. It is just a matter of awareness and consciousness. You are only limited in your abilities by your own set beliefs and expectations. If your beliefs grow and widen, then so do your abilities to contact beings on all different levels. Perhaps with this thought of your potential ability to contact us at all levels of being, I have shared with you enough for this morning. You may have many questions from what I have said and I will happily try to answer these questions if you ask me to do so. Meantime all blessings. Yours ever, **Philip.**

QUESTIONS

Bob   Philip, are you ready and willing to answer my questions this morning?

Philip   Bob my brother, I am both ready and willing, and will answer your questions to the best of my ability, God willing.

Bob   Philip, many people may find it strange, or even fanciful, that I am holding a conversation with you as my Guardian Angel. They may think that in reality such a thing is not really possible. Is it?

Philip   Bob, my brother in Spirit, you know that it is possible and that we are doing this now. The Angel assigned to each person knows that person intimately. His or her higher Being is known by the Angel. So is it really so surprising that we can communicate, since we are actually so closely intertwined?

Bob   Nonetheless Philip, many people would still think that all this talk of angels, especially perhaps Guardian Angels, is just so much wishful thinking encouraged by religions, myths and dogma.

Philip   They may of course think that, but this does not change the actual reality. Guardian Angels are as 'concrete', so to speak, as your husband or wife, or your friend or neighbour. We are there for you, to give the support, guidance and protection that you need.

Bob   Philip, you talk about giving protection but, if this is true, why do people still end up sometimes in dangerous, even life-threatening situations?

Philip   We cannot interfere with peoples' free will. If they choose to do this or that, and this then puts them in harm's way, then all we can do is to help as much as we can. We cannot interfere in your own decisions.

Bob   Alright Philip, I can accept this, but what if people end up in situations not of their own choosing and find themselves in danger?

Philip   Truth be told, people choose to be at a certain place at a certain time in order to have certain experiences which they need. Sometimes this puts them deliberately in harm's way.

Bob   Now with this idea many people would I'm sure, disagree with you. They would say that in no way could people, let's say caught up in a terrorist incident, have chosen that situation. It's just bad luck.

Philip Yes, it appears to be just bad luck but, nonetheless, in your higher Self, your Spirit Being, you do direct yourselves to where your karma takes you. Even though, in your ordinary self, you have no knowledge of this.

Bob   So are you really saying that nothing takes place by chance and that everything in a person's life is pre-planned?

Philip Yes, I am saying that, even though I know that many people will have difficulty accepting this.

Bob   But Philip, if things are really pre-planned then what of human freedom, choice and free decisions?

Philip But you have made your choices before you were born on Earth. You have yourself already planned out the course of your life, and what lessons you need to learn to balance out your karmic debts.

Bob   Philip, it seems to me that this is very tricky, sensitive ground to tread upon, considering what difficult, or even awful, situations people can find themselves in.

Philip Yes you are right my friend and brother, it is difficult ground but, nonetheless, it is true that you yourselves are the architects of your fate, of your destinies.

Bob Let us turn to another question. You talk about angels as well as humans moving along an evolutionary path and that, for angels, they progress through a life of service. Can you say more about this?

Philip Yes I can. We live a life of service in order to please God. We are part of the Divine Plan and we are thankful to play our part, in ministering to our human brethren. Our whole life is dedicated to that purpose. Through serving our human brothers we advance through the angelic ranks as it were. Over the aeons we make progress in the sense that we are given higher responsibilities to carry. We then take on these new tasks with joy and devotion.

Bob But Philip, are you therefore saying that after a certain time you no longer need to protect, guard, a particular human being? And if so, what then happens to that person?

Philip Our destinies, so to speak, are intertwined. If, in time, the human being in our care makes sufficient progress towards his/her own Spirit recognition and realisation, then we do not need to exercise the same care and concern for them. They can take full responsibility for their own onward journey and we are free, so to speak, to pursue our journey also. This only happens when it is sanctioned by higher powers, by more knowledgeable and wise Spirit Beings who oversee the work of the angelic kingdom.

Bob How long does it take a human being to set his/her Guardian Angel free?

Philip Many thousands of years in your earth time. It is a lengthy process and one that cannot be rushed or hurried.

Bob   Are such human beings highly developed spiritually?

Philip   Yes they are and that is why it takes so many thousands of years to reach that level of attainment.

Bob   Philip, coming back to basics, many people perhaps will not believe in angels per se. How can they receive any evidence that could convince them that they have a Guardian Angel?

Philip   The evidence is there for them all the time if they would but open their eyes and see it. In countless ways the angels are working to help their human beings through their lives to fulfil their chosen destinies.

Bob   But how can a person see this?

Philip   They can see it when they begin to notice in how many ways they are given a helping hand, so to speak. In how many instances something comes along to help them to get from A to B. To give them a helpful sign or feeling, 'Yes, this is what I'd better do now' or 'No, this is not a good idea.' It is a question of noticing what is working in your day-to-day life and helping you along.

Bob   Alright Philip, but what about people who choose to do great harm to others? I have to think here of the recent terrorist acts and those who perpetrated them.

Philip   The angels, their Angels, are filled with sorrow when such people do harm to others. Angels want only the good, they never sanction harm or hatred. The angels will do all they can to turn people away from wrong-doing, but, as I say, we cannot interfere with your free will even when that free will is used to inflict harm on others.

Bob Philip, we need to draw to a close, but one final question. How can we best connect and contact our own particular Guardian Angel? How to practically do this?

Philip By prayer and meditation. By stilling your mind and coming to peace in yourselves, so that you can be sensitive to our presence. Imagine that each Angel stands behind his/her brother and sister, and lays his hands on your shoulders. Feel the peace and blessing which this can bring to you, to know that you are held and cared for. Cared for unconditionally. Cared for day and night. Your Angel is always there for you, even if you feel bereft of physical friends or companions. Your Angel will never abandon you, but remains faithful to the task which has been entrusted to him. Learn to feel this trust, learn to feel that you are watched over every step of the way. God loves you and it is God's love that unites us with you all. All blessings, **Philip**.

Bob Thank you Philip.

12

A REFLECTIVE REVIEW

I began to write this Review some six weeks since receiving the last Communication with Spirit. Namely, the 'Question and Answer' session with Philip on 6 June 2017.

In reading through all the communications received, prior to starting this final chapter, I was impressed with the clarity and forthrightness of the contents from the Guides. As I read each contribution I made notes about the main points raised in that particular Guide's Teachings. This simple analytic process then made it easy to compare my notes, over the totality of all the teachings.

This research strategy showed that there were some definite 'themes' that emerged, as important topics common to two or more of the Guides. Of course there were also other important points which were specific to a Spirit Guide and not echoed by others in this more thematic sense. A good example of this was the specifically health-related issues, which formed the substance of John's teachings.

However, for this chapter, I will just identify certain common themes, and reflect upon them. But before doing so it is worthwhile pointing out to you the marked contrast between my own thinking about these Teachings and the receipt of 'ready-made' channelled thoughts. The latter flowed into my mind quite effortlessly and with continuity, whereas to now exercise my own reflective thinking requires a real effort on my part! This contrast highlights, for me at least, the genuine experience of receiving telepathic communications from Spirit.

Interestingly, this same contrast also applies in the field of pictures and images. There is a great difference between doing deliberate visualisations and, instead, being receptive to images given from Spirit on the 'mind-screen'. Having said this, let us now turn to some of the main themes found in the Teachings and reflect upon them, albeit only briefly.

1. 'YOU ARE SPIRIT-BEINGS'

This statement from Red Cloud is also echoed in the teachings given by Pierre and Raja Lampa. It is also implied by the other Guides when they speak about us having set our own goals and aims, for this current earthly life, before our birth. It is a concept widely found in the literature on spirituality and Spiritual Healing.

I am especially familiar with the body of research findings provided by Rudolf Steiner in his Anthroposophy, where the essential spiritual core of our Being is pointed to again and again. Raja Lampa says that, 'Spirit lies deep within each human soul' and is the 'eternal kernel within the soul.' So the notion that we are not simply physical, material beings of flesh and blood, but also, and actually much more essentially, beings of soul and spirit, begs serious consideration. Not least because this would mean that we cannot, in reality, be reduced by a materialistic viewpoint to an accumulation of cells, genes and body-chemistry. This biological view amounts to only a part of our multi-layered, multi-dimensional, human nature. In his clairvoyant investigations as presented in his book *Theosophy*, Steiner, for example, speaks of nine distinct 'members' of the human constitution. These include three spirit parts, three soul parts, and three bodily parts. The latter are the so-called physical, etheric, and astral bodies. By virtue of these different constituent members of our Being, we have an affinity for different levels of existence or, we could say, for 'higher worlds' above the physical plane. A truly holistic model of the human being, as underpins Steiner's anthroposophy, must therefore embrace the physical, soul, and spiritual levels, though of these the Spirit is really the essential core of our innermost Being.

This core concept can illuminate our understanding of such well-known phenomena as NDEs (Near Death Experiences) and OBEs (Out of Body Experiences). The NDEs began to be highlighted since the 1970s through books by Dr Raymond Moody, George Ritchie, and others. All such experiences seem to strongly suggest that our individual consciousness and awareness transcends direct dependence on the physical body and the brain. In other words, our consciousness is not obliterated with the death of our material body, but lives on in a 'body-free' condition. Or, to return to Red Cloud's assertion, 'You are Spirit-beings'. This leads us on to another main theme.

2. 'YOU SET YOUR OWN LESSONS'

You set your own lessons before birth, was described by Philip, Red Cloud, John and Joshua. This theme is intimately connected with setting our own aims and goals for our current life on Earth, with the intention of realising our self-chosen destiny or mission. Philip, the Angel, described 'Life as a School' in which people move 'from stage to stage' as lessons are learnt and goals achieved. However, this whole idea of setting lessons which we need, so that we can progress and spiritually evolve, raises tricky issues and problems. Of course it is true that life often teaches us that, in order to achieve some goal or learn a new skill, we have to exert ourselves and confront obstacles and challenges. Nonetheless, it can be very much more difficult to see anything particularly positive when major pitfalls befall us. Say, a serious accident or a life-changing illness.

To then imagine that we ourselves, as a Spirit-being, have intentionally orchestrated such blows of fate can be hard to swallow. 'No way would I have wished this chronic illness, or this horrific car accident, upon myself!' Yet even in these difficult circumstances, and actually just because of them, we can often learn things about ourselves which would otherwise have been impossible. When we can acknowledge this, in spite of all, then a feeling of gratitude may arise for the wisdom of our destiny. Indeed, we sometimes hear of other people who, having been faced with painful life-changing events, surmount their infirmities and show great courage and fortitude. They often admit that they have become better, perhaps less selfish people, precisely because of what life has faced them with. Such people can then become role-models for others to follow and, in such instances, the notion of premeditated events to help a person's inner development, appears much more plausible. Though, having said this, others may 'sink', rather than rise to meet life's challenges and opportunities! So the notion of pre-natal aims and plans, can remain a complex and tricky issue when viewed from this earthly side of life. However, these 'destiny' considerations form a natural link to a theme emerging in the Teachings from Dr John and Philip, namely, the concepts of:

3. KARMA AND REINCARNATION

Karma, an Indian term derived from Sanskrit, is usually taken to mean the connection between actions done in one lifetime, or incarnation, and the subsequent one. It is seen as a spiritual law of 'cause and effect', so that deeds done in one life will reap consequences for the next. Therefore the concepts of karma and reincarnation are intimately intertwined. Perhaps, for example, a person's malicious deeds will later lead to some illness or infirmity in a future life? On the other hand, good deeds may reap manifold blessings in the next incarnation. In the traditional structure of Indian society 'good karma' permitted progression from a lower to a higher caste from life to life.

Belief in reincarnation and karma is deeply rooted in Eastern religions, especially in Hinduism and its off-shoots. Apparently much Hindu religious thought and practice is directed towards the clearing of karma accumulated from **past** actions. This emphasis gives the impression that the Eastern outlook tends to a fatalistic, passive, attitude towards a person's present circumstances in life. Or, to put it more plainly, you've now got exactly what you deserve due to your past karma! In a sense, the human being was seen as trapped in a recurring cycle of deaths and rebirths, in a 'Great Wheel' of earthly lives. Spiritual advancement was the way to liberate oneself from this ongoing repetition, and finally escape from the necessity of having to reincarnate again.

There is, however, also a very different approach possible towards karma, one that is much more proactive and futuristic. Namely, rather than being held back or simply conditioned by old or past karma, to **now** do everything possible in the present to purposely create new future benefits. This is the opposite of any sort of fatalism and is much more optimistic and hopeful. It is also evolutionary in nature, so that instead of 'a wheel' of deaths and rebirths, the image of an upward-going 'spiral' is much more appropriate.

I think that a good example of this positive attitude to active karma creation is shown by my experiences, spanning forty years, within the Steiner-inspired Camphill school setting. Living and working there with children with Special Needs, some of them severe, the approach was to deliberately intervene to try to change things for the better. By 'better', I mean out of a recognition of each child's inner potentials as an evolving human being. Whilst karmic, spiritual, laws do need to be fulfilled, the actual ways in which this can be achieved are various. This allows for ethical interventions into the karmic situation of another person, such as happened daily in the field of anthroposophical curative education. Even if only small improvements were seen in this lifetime, these could have very real significance for a future incarnation.

Whilst normally we do not think of traditional Christian teachings, within the orthodox Churches, as including notions of reincarnation and karma per se, nonetheless I feel that a broader Christian viewpoint can encompass these concepts, particularly in a healing and redemptive sense towards new future possibilities. There are also examples to be found, even within the Gospel narratives, that suggest an awareness of reincarnation and the links of karma. For example, in St John's gospel the issue of the man who was born blind, when the disciples asked Jesus whether he or his parents had sinned as the cause for his infirmity. Since he was said to be 'born blind' how could **he** possibly have been responsible for his impairment, unless he had existed already before his present birth? Perhaps in a previous incarnation?

The ancient Indian teachings concerning karma and reincarnation now need to be seen and understood in a modern context. Indeed, one of Rudolf Steiner's most important tasks as a spiritual-researcher was to investigate, newly, the workings of karma and reincarnation. He clearly presented his findings in many of his books and lectures. For example, the eleven lectures given in Hamburg in 1910, *The Manifestations of Karma*, give important insights into a whole range of scenarios, including; illness and diseases, accidents, earthquakes and volcanoes, freewill and human evolution. Steiner believed that it was very important that the truths of reincarnation and karma would penetrate modern culture and, in doing so, essentially transform it. This was already in the early 20th century! My understanding based on anthroposophy is also that, since the events of the first Easter, the karmic situation is significantly different than it was in earlier pre-Christian ages. With its redemptive and transformative power of Cosmic Love, the Christ-Impulse has changed the ways in which karma can be balanced and made good for the Earth. However, we cannot go further into this important subject here. Karmic relationships, and specific past reincarnations, are complex matters and they need careful clairvoyant investigations to fathom them correctly. This is therefore a subject that can easily be prone to various misinterpretations and errors. That said, probably all of us have sometimes met someone whom we felt we already knew well, like seeing an 'old friend'. This may perhaps point us back toward a former relationship in a past earthly life?

While we cannot change the past, ours or the World's, we can most certainly start to create the future in the present moment. The karmic future does, quite literally, lie in our own hands much more than we may realise. This may also include group, and even National, karmic situations. In a time when many believe that human beings are largely, if not completely determined by their genetic constitution and code, it is salutary to reflect on our innate spirituality. If it is true that we, as Spirit-beings, are instrumental in choosing the lessons we require in our earthly lives, then we cannot put our behaviours and actions, and choices, simply down to genetic determinism. A 21st century knowledge of reincarnation and karma can provide a richer and deeper sense of meaning and purpose to the colourful tapestry of our individual lives, and the many challenges which we face.

Let us now turn to a rather different theme.

4. MOTHER EARTH AND THE NATURE KINGDOMS

This environmental theme is central to Pan's contributions, but also Pierre and Joshua highlight our responsibilities in 'shaping the World' and bringing about 'health and wellbeing of the whole planet.' Pan's emphasis is for people to show respect, reverence, and humility, for Mother Earth, instead of being driven by greed and egotism. Both he and Pierre speak about spirit-beings who actively care for the vitality of the planet; particularly the various Nature Spirits and Elemental Beings. There is, it seems, an urgent need for humans to cooperate with these beings. The whole planet, Mother Earth, is a living, breathing, vital organism, rather than any 'imagined' dead, mineral globe. The Earth, they say, has a Soul and Spirit nature in addition to her physical body.

She suffers in her very Being through selfish human exploitation, rampant pollution, and blatant disregard for the delicate balance of the interconnected Nature Kingdoms. We have all heard about the decimation of large areas of the tropical rain forests, about the extinction of certain animal species, and the creation of dust-bowls through the erosion of the living soil. These, and many other depletions of our natural resources, are all man-made. Pan describes so-called natural disasters as 'wake-up calls' to individuals, Nations and their governments, to recognise their responsibilities as 'custodians of the Earth', for this and future generations.

It surely does not need much reflection about these Teachings for us to know that care of our natural environment is in everyone's best interest. No doubt this ecological awareness and responsibility needs to be fostered from childhood, through education and example, and by cultivating a love of Nature in all its forms. The incredible life-work of Sir David Attenborough in raising our consciousness for the Kingdoms of Nature and their mutual interplay cannot be overstated. As the Spirit Guides say, if everyone begins to care for their local and immediate surroundings then this has benefits for the whole World. Let us hope that the current drive to reduce plastic pollution, especially in our oceans, will spur us all to take decisive actions and to feel responsible for our precious planet.

Moreover, as Pan points out to us, countless invisible beings work tirelessly to sustain our natural world on all levels. This is not simply the stuff of fairy tales and mythologies, but a reality in which we are constantly immersed. This reality has long been known to native and indigenous peoples, whose very survival depended on a respect and cooperation with their natural surroundings. The time has come for a reawakening of our awareness of the Nature Spirits and the Elemental Beings. Love for Mother Earth is the surest way to cultivate this consciousness anew, together with a sense of wonder and gratitude for Nature in all her incredible manifoldness.

5. PRAYER AND MEDITATION

This theme emerges in the teachings from Markos, Raja Lampa, and Philip. The inward, spiritual, activity implicit in the terms prayer and meditation is seen by these Guides as the way, the means, to connect with Spirit realities of being. For example, Markos speaks about 'building bridges' from the physical to the Spirit Worlds, Raja Lampa of connecting to our own 'Spirit-Selves', and Philip as the way to contact our 'Guardian Angels'.

Traditionally, prayer appears as a practice embedded in Western spirituality and conventional religions, whereas meditation is seen as very much belonging to the wisdom of the East. It is interesting to contrast the typical gestures of these two practices. In prayer the kneeling supplicant places the palms of the hands together, with fingers pointing upwards. The Eastern meditant sits with the soles of the feet upturned in the Lotus posture and, sometimes at least, with opened palms. These typical gestures could perhaps suggest that in prayer we connect ourselves strongly to the Earth whilst petitioning God's help, while in Eastern meditation the upturned feet indicate a desire to liberate ourselves from the earth-sphere, to seek bliss in Nirvana? However this simple comparison is not intended to rigidly stereotype prayer and meditation, nor Western and Eastern practices. Nowadays, in terms of contemporary spirituality, I think both these disciplines transcend East and West and specific cultures and set traditions. The essential point of both is that, through them, people aim to connect, or reconnect, to universal spirituality and/or to their own Spirit core. If you like, to God without, and the god within.

It was during the 1960s and 1970s, with the advent of the so-called 'New Age', that there came about a strong movement towards Eastern spirituality and a turning to Indian gurus and yogis for guidance. The Beatles and their association with Maharishi Mahesh Yogi epitomised the trend of the time. No doubt this trend, which included 'the hippies', 'flower power', 'pot', and the use of psychedelic substances, was symptomatic of a genuine searching for values and meaning beyond Western materialism and capitalism.

Today it is very much the practice of 'Mindfulness', with its Zen Buddhist origins, that attracts the popular imagination. This is often seen as a way to overcome the considerable tensions and stresses of modern life, by learning to be fully there in 'the present moment'. So, when the Guides point us towards prayer and meditation the obvious question is, 'What should we choose to do, out of the wide variety of techniques on offer?' There is no shortage of books on these subjects, particularly meditation practices. When I put this question to Markos he replied that, 'Each person, each individual, needs to find what speaks to them. Here your Guides can be helpful if you ask them to guide you along the right, or best track, shall we say.' But he also later added, 'They will do all they can to help whilst respecting your free will and your choices in life.'

In my experience, prayer and meditation is an ongoing journey, and it is a daily challenge to engage, fully, in this inner activity. However it can also be felt as a sort of 'free-necessity', not only to deal with all the outer pressures but also to provide a deeper sense of meaning and purpose in one's life. I suppose if I was asked to give advice about meditation I would say, 'Keep it simple, rather than complicated and, above all, enter into it with the right feeling and motivation.'

It is also possible to unite with other like-minded people through meditative practice, for some higher common purpose, say, to direct Healing to the whole World. With these thoughts I will pass on to another theme, but one which is directly connected to the above, namely:

6. THE HEART AS A SOURCE OF WISDOM

This theme was especially pointed to by Markos and Red Cloud.

Markos spoke of the heart's innate Wisdom in reference to urgent questions and riddles which life presents us with. Answers, he said, can be found in 'the depths of our own hearts'. But, how can this be done? According to Markos, by learning to listen and to tune-in to what we already have within us. The key to this, he says, 'Is found in prayer and meditation'. Red Cloud also points to the knowledge of the heart and, in answer to a question, refers to a new form of perception in your heart. He says, 'The World-Word sounds out in your own hearts and souls.'

Poets have often referred to the heart as the centre of our life of feelings and emotions, and especially so of romantic love. There are many common phrases which point to the heart's emotional and intentional role in our lives. For example, we speak of being of 'good heart', or, instead, of being 'cold hearted', or 'half-hearted'. To 'wear one's heart on one's sleeve' is to show one's feelings openly, whilst to have a 'heart of gold' indicates much goodwill and kindness. However, what the Guides are referring to here has I think little or nothing to do with those emotions which can also easily confuse us and muddy both thoughts and perceptions. Far rather it is a more subtle level of our soul and intentional life, that is intended here.

Whereas our mind can often be buzzing with all manner of thoughts and images, and strong emotions can surge through us like restless waves in the sea, to really listen to the heart's depths requires some inner stillness and peace. If this inner listening activity is cultivated then, perhaps, the answers we seek will arise and bring us new clarity and direction? At any event, this 'wisdom of the heart' is surely a resource to be tapped into rather than ignored. Which again brings us back to prayer and meditation as ways to tune-in to our own spirit depths, to our own, wiser, Spirit Being. Perhaps we could visualise going into 'The Room of our Heart', as our own inner sacred sanctuary, to find wisdom and peace?

The next theme takes us far beyond our small, limited, everyday ego.

7. CONSCIOUSNESS AND LIFE IN THE COSMOS

Both Markos and Philip speak of consciousness as operating throughout the universe. Philip elaborates on this by referring to 'Many ranks of Beings' and says that the universe 'teams with life and consciousness' on many levels. This description is, perhaps, a far cry from the lifeless immensities of space and time that modern cosmology portrays. (Though there are also those scientists who, I believe, think that many planets capable of supporting life may be extant throughout the cosmos.) Perhaps we can also see the Guides' assertions in the context of their reference to 'Spirit Worlds'? That is to say, of worlds, or levels of life, which are not bound to matter or physicality as we understand it.

In terms of where these worlds, ranks of Beings, or levels of life and consciousness, are to be found, I suspect they are already within our reach, at least potentially! Instead of needing bigger and more powerful rockets to shoot us or our technology into distant space and time, might it not be that an ability to deliberately alter our own states of consciousness is really what is needed? If our consciousness is sufficiently heightened, or raised, then quite new perceptions and a greatly expanded awareness may be experienced. Phenomena such as so-called 'astral travelling' and 'out of body experiences' (OBEs) are well-known, if still not well understood. In such states, the everyday 'realities' can be transcended and we can become aware of different dimensions of reality beyond the limitations of our usual five senses. When I work with my friend Neil to do our spirit-research sessions it is necessary that we both raise our energies consciously. Rudolf Steiner speaks about the ability to leave the physical body at will, and to still remain awake, in order to do actual spiritual investigations. Moreover, whether it is really a matter of lots of different, separate worlds or levels, a sort of multiverse, or actually a Cosmic One-ness where many beings and planes co-exist, is a valid question to consider and explore. Philip said that, 'Beings are not separate in your physical, bodily sense. They interpenetrate and form a complete oneness or wholeness.' Philosophically, this is a One-World or monistic viewpoint. Altogether, questions about the nature of consciousness per se, continues to be a field of much current research.

8. THE POWER OF LOVE

Nearly all the Guides refer to love as the most important power in the universe. John, giving his teachings from the perspective of his healing vocation, points out that, 'Love is the most essential nourishment for all human beings.' He makes clear that what he means by love, has nothing to do with self-gratification, but that in its true form it is, 'the substance that sustains all life in your world and ours.' In answer to a question, John added that, 'Love is the source of all life-forms, both on planet Earth and in the Cosmos as a whole.' Suchlike thoughts and teachings were echoed by the other Guides.

The word 'love' is however often used by people in ways that are remote from this pure and creative universal life-force. Perhaps far too often it is degraded by sheer sexuality, and confused by so-called 'love-making' in the most physical of senses only. However in its true meaning, love is really an expression of pure compassion, empathy, and selflessness. The very opposite, therefore, of narrow egotism and simple self-gratification.

The fact that love is such a clear-cut common theme for the Spirit Guides indicates its fundamental importance for all life and on all levels of being. Pierre speaks of this universal power in connection with Nature and Mother Earth when he says that, 'Love for Nature, love for all that the Earth provides, love for the blessings which the Earth daily gives us, will strengthen peoples' resolve to do all they can to love the planet. That is to love the soul and spirit, the Being, of the planet.'

This is then taken a step further by Pan when he refers to the 'Cosmic Christ' as 'the Lord of Life' and asks us to,

> 'Let His love, which is also the power of Life, stream through you, and then the planet, Mother Earth, that is, will also be filled with new life.'

In Steiner's anthroposophy the deeds of Christ on Golgotha are seen as the unique pivotal point in the entire course of World-evolution. Through them, the Christ as the Cosmic Sun-Spirit united Himself with humanity and the Earth per se.

It is not too difficult to imagine how different the whole world would be, and especially our different cultures and societies, if the real power of Christ's universal love would stream through us human beings, no matter what our particular creed, colour, or political leanings.

Is this grand Imagination nothing more than an unattainable utopia or pipe-dream, or is it actually an ever present potential that waits to be grounded through each individual – through us? Grounded not in any sentimental or emotionally-charged sense, but as a source of life, compassion, empathy, and true humanity. Very much, I feel, in line with the teachings of His Holiness the Dalai Lama, since each enlightened person helps to transform the whole World.

Perhaps the clearest definition of the power of love is to be found in the First Letter of St Paul to the Corinthians when he writes,

'Love is patient; love is kind and envies no one. Love is never boastful, nor conceited, nor rude; never selfish, not quick to take offence. Love keeps no score of wrongs; does not gloat over other men's sins, but delights in the Truth. There is nothing love cannot face; there is no limit to its faith, its hope, and its endurance.'

(1 Cor.13. 4-7 New English Bible)

These words are certainly very challenging for us to try to live up to!

9. SPIRIT GUIDES

This is the last common theme that I will reflect upon here and, in the context of this book, it is the most obvious one of all. After all, the main chapters are provided not by me, but by each of the Guides speaking in turn. That they want to share their teachings is the very reason the book exists. Nonetheless, even if readers agree that these Teachings, on reflection, do make a lot of sense and also the answers to the various questions, were they really given by Spirit Guides? Might not Bob Woodward himself be a man of 'many parts', rather like an actor playing different roles? Perhaps, in the language of psychosynthesis, giving expression to his sub-personalities?

I can only reply to this conjecture by pointing out that it was very much easier, and a good deal quicker, to consciously receive and record the Communications than to formulate my own chapters for this book! The actual experience of 'receiving', rather than 'thinking through' contents was an evident and experiential contrast for me. You must, of course, as reader, explain that contrast as you will, but I would certainly say that *Trusting in Spirit – the Challenge* is the interpretation that I unequivocally accept. Not that this doesn't continue to amaze me, because it does. However I have long been convinced that reality is much stranger than fiction!

In the Introduction to the book entitled **Staying Connected** which contains selected talks and meditations by Rudolf Steiner, we read that,

'Those who have passed through the gates of death want to work with us on the physical world. This working together only appears to be a physical collaboration, for everything physical is only an outer expression of spirit. Materialism has alienated human beings from the world of the dead. Spiritual science must help us to make friends again with that world.'

I have never liked the terms 'the dead' or 'the world of the dead', since there is certainly nothing dead about life in spirit worlds. However, Steiner clearly anticipated a more conscious cooperation with our friends across the threshold, even if, to my knowledge, he did not use the actual expression 'Spirit Guides'.

If then it is indeed true that each one of us has Spirit Guides, it surely makes sense to try to establish conscious contact and communication with them. Throughout this book the Guides have made it abundantly clear that they are there, and very willing to be of help, support and encouragement to us. Bearing in mind of course that they need **to be asked**, before giving any help or advice. True Guides always respect our own free will and will not interfere in our choices and decisions. This spiritual law also applies to our very own Guardian Angel who, following Divine Will, is our constant companion through the course of our earthly incarnations. For those who are really interested to begin to establish a conscious rapport with their Guides I can thoroughly recommend the recent volume by the internationally-known medium James Van Praagh, which is included in my Bibliography. Interestingly, he also makes reference to Rudolf Steiner in his book's Introduction. I feel that what James describes therein also serves to further validate my own experiences with my Guides.

Within the context of my present book it is those experiences, and especially the Teachings thereby received, which are more important than simply my own reflections.

I will close this Review by quoting words which came through at the end of my *Spirit Communications* ten years ago:

'Love lives in the light and in the light the power of love holds sway when angel messengers unite with thoughts of men to bring the world to harmony and to peace.'

Postscript:

The teachings contained in this book were received during that period of time when awful terrorist acts took place in Manchester and London in the UK, and also during Summer 2017 when forest fires raged in various European countries and the USA. In the light, or rather darkness, of such destructive events, the Guides' contributions are, I think, both timely and urgent to consider. It seems to me that we need all the help we can get from our friends in Spirit, including the Angels, if we are to succeed in making our World a safer and happier place for our grandchildren, and their children, to live in.

Dr Bob Woodward

THE AUTHOR

I was born in 1947 in Gloucester in the UK. At the age of eleven I had the good fortune to fail my 11-plus exam, which was then the entrance into what sort of State secondary education was available to pupils. Through this stroke of destiny, I entered 'Wynstones' an independent Rudolf Steiner School in Gloucestershire, where I remained for seven years until I was eighteen. Following 'A levels' in Maths and Physics I went to University and, a year later, became a university drop-out!

At the age of twenty-three, at Easter 1970, I was guided to become a co-worker at the Sheiling School in Thornbury, a centre of the Camphill Community, based on the teachings of Rudolf Steiner (1861-1925). Apart from a year at Emerson College in Sussex, I spent some forty years within the Camphill Movement, living with and teaching children with Special Educational Needs. I retired from this work in 2012.

I became a student of Steiner's 'Anthroposophy', having first read one of his fundamental books, *Knowledge of the Higher Worlds – how is it achieved?* when I was around eighteen years old, now more than fifty years ago. Later I also became a member of the Anthroposophical Society in Great Britain. I have however always tried to keep an open-mind, and I consider myself a perpetual student. When I was forty-six I received an M.Ed degree from Bristol University and this was followed by an M.Phil when I was fifty. In 2011, I was awarded a Ph.D from the University of the West of England, when nearly sixty-four.

As well as being a qualified Curative Educator, I am also a Spiritual Healer and an author. I took a special interest in understanding autism in children and young people.

I have a lifelong interest in philosophy and spirituality, and in exploring the existential questions of life and death, meaning and freedom. Fundamentally I see myself as a researcher in the field of spirituality, particularly in my conscious relationships with my Spirit Guides over the past twelve years and my ongoing work with them.

In 2018 I will have been married for forty years, to Silke my wife. We have five grown-up children and, currently, ten lively grandchildren. I enjoy walking, swimming, reading, writing, painting, and pram-pushing! My wife and I particularly look forward to our holidays on the beautiful Isles of Scilly in Cornwall.

I feel that I have received clear guidance in my own life, and am very grateful for this.

A SELECT BIBILOGRAPHY

Wisdom from your Spirit Guides (2017)
by James Van Praagh. Hay House.

Working with Spirit Guides (2004)
by Ruth White. Piatkus.

Summer with the Leprechauns (1997)
by Tanis Helliwel. Blue Dolphin Publishing.

Nature Spirits and What They say (2004)
by Verena Stael von Holstein. Floris Books.

Encounters with Pan and the Elemental Kingdom (2009)
by R. Ogilvie Crombie. Double CD. Findhorn Press.

Working with Angels, Fairies and Nature Spirits (2003)
by William Bloom. Piatkus.

Angels in My Hair (2009)
by Lorna Byrne. Arrow Books.

Stairways to Heaven (2011)
by Lorna Byrne. Coronet.

The Voices of Angels (2012)
by Francesca Brown. Hodder.

Life After Life (1975)
by Raymond A. Moody. Bantam Books.

Theosophy (1994)
by Rudolf Steiner. Rudolf Steiner Press.

Reincarnation and Karma (1977)
by Rudolf Steiner. Rudolf Steiner Press.

Manifestations of Karma (2000)
by Rudolf Steiner. Rudolf Steiner Press.

How to Know Higher Worlds (1994)
by Rudolf Steiner. Anthroposophic Press.

Staying Connected (1999)
edited by Christopher Bamford. Anthroposophic Press.

Reincarnation in Modern Life (1997)
by Pietro Archiati. Temple Lodge.

Spirit Communications (2007)
by Bob Woodward. Athena Press.

Spiritual Healing with Children with Special Needs (2007)
by Bob Woodward. Jessica Kingsley.

AFTERWORD

A week before Christmas 2017 and six months or so since I completed the manuscript of this book, I decided to write to Anne Lewis, my spiritual medium friend in Yorkshire. I wanted to ask her if she was willing to do a Reading for me, in which she would ask each of the eight Guides who has contributed to the book if they had any advice, or message, for me and perhaps also for Anne herself. Now I could, of course, have asked the Guides myself this same question, but I was interested to see how they might come through to Anne, knowing from previous contact that her way of receiving impressions was rather different from my telepathic direct line. In particular she received visual impressions and pictures, as metaphors or similes, in a way that, normally, I don't. Depending on Anne's willingness to do this and the nature of the content received, I already thought that perhaps this could form an 'Afterword' to be included in the book. However I did not mention any such possibility to Anne at that time.

Christmas came and went and I had not yet received the Reading from Anne, which I expected as usual in a small package containing the tape. On Sunday 14 January I decided to give Anne a ring at her home to see how she was and enquire about the request I had made in December. She was now well and told me that she planned to do the Reading for me early next week. When I subsequently received it, it was dated 16 January 2018. On listening to it I had no doubts that it would be helpful to include this in the form of an Afterword. Therefore I lost no time in carefully transcribing the words of the tape-recording onto paper. They read as follows below:

'Today's date is 16 January 2018. My name is Anne Lewis, I am a Spiritual Medium, and this is a Reading for Bob.'

Right, 'Greetings Anne, it is a while since we met to share our mediumistic abilities.' This is Joshua and he said he's the one who's managing to draw together those who shared your journey through your book, to give a little inspiration or clarification, in a way that is interesting to you. And I think the questions you wanted to ask each of your Guides was if they have any particular advice for you at this time or indeed something they simply wish to share, perhaps with you and I.

Right **Joshua**, is there anything that you could; 'I advise Bob to sit tight, his book will be published when the time is right. There is indeed a market out there, although they say it is a niche market, it is one that will be absorbed well. If we could wave a wand, like Harry Potter, then we could have the books appear on your table, then their production would give you less satisfaction than they will when you have worked to get them published.' Now I've just seen a foot, and a shoe is being put on the foot, but the foot is too small for the shoe, and the shoe has just come off. And with this Joshua is saying that the niche market is the right fitting foot to go in the shoe. And sometimes you have to try on a few shoes before you find the one that's the perfect fit, even if they all advertise the same size. There is one that is uniquely fitted to the job. Now I'm seeing someone, I think the saying is 'no stone unturned', because somebody is picking up a stone and looking underneath it. So I suggest that even if you have to delve a little deeper, and Joshua's loving all these little sayings that are coming out, because it fits in well with the Jewish tradition of sayings and stories, often repeated.

Now I think he's saying, 'Don't worry about time' because I'm being shown an oven and a cake is being put in the oven. And because the cake is wanted quickly, the oven is turned up high, and the cake is burned and is not fit for consumption. Whereas if you wait, with the perfect temperature and the perfect timing, then the cake that you take out is sweet, and fulfils its purpose of nourishment. So I think here Joshua is telling you not to be disheartened Bob, but to keep plugging along until you find the right publisher. I think you'll be directed there, because I was shown which stone to pick up and look under, so it's almost as if you will have the same encouragement as to which publisher to go to. Now I don't know why but I've just seen 'a cock', as in a hen, and the only association I can get with that, was it 'bantam', is there a bantam cock? Maybe that's something to look out for, because I was going to say that the only cockerel that I knew was one that was for a brewery, and I think that was down South somewhere. But then I just said 'bantam' and I think there is a Bantam Press. Okay, thank you for that Joshua, anything else? Says, 'No, let's carry on and go through the list for all that's required.'

Dr John, welcome. I see Dr John in shirt sleeves rolled up and trousers and see him perching on the healing bed, very casual and relaxed. He's been doing a lot of work in Spirit because there is much to attend to and much that is coming your way. I think he means the general population here, not specific. So I feel he's been working on advancements that will come through to the medical profession. And I'm just trying to focus to ask him, 'What areas are you working on?' Okay, what I'm getting is nothing specific, it is something that will be, I think it will be a 'breakthrough' that will help a vast amount of people rather than, for example, one specific drug or idea that would help a few people. This is something that, a shift, so are we talking genetics, or? They're working on how to get an understanding through to the people who do research, and I think we're talking about Alzheimer's, dementia-type things here. It's something that the doctors in Spirit have seen how this can help, or it can be linked, it's like the next step in the treatment cum prevention of dementia, Alzheimer's. Dr John has been working with a big team to try to get it into a format that can be plopped into somebody's head, to their understanding. And it's more the practicalities, I feel, that Dr John's been working on, maybe that's why he's not wearing his white coat because he's been doing something theoretical. He said research is vitally important and Spirit have a lot of input in medical research, it's just a matter of – and I can see ideas dripping from Spirit into the human mind – doing this in a way that the human can absorb it. Thank you Dr John, will look forward to – I've just seen a clock, so it's time – so what's the time? Time to diagnosis, is that what we're saying, from initial – it's how to early diagnose. So look out for that research, because it's taking me back to the lady that can smell Parkinson's that was on the television the other night, and it's something like that where she can smell it and the science behind that is being delved into. Thank you for that. Dr John is there anything else? No, I don't feel there is anything else.

Now **Markos**. I've just said the name 'Markos' and someone has just stood before me and bowed the head in acknowledgement and respect. Markos it's lovely to meet you and accept you into our home. Bob is asking if you have any particular advice for him at this time, or something that you simply wish to share?

I'm getting the impression that, okay, he's suggesting I think, because I'm struggling to receive a communication with him, that I'm actually receiving the communication; so is it my perception of not receiving it properly? 'We are not accustomed to be communicating together. And as when we meet strangers, we meet with respect and an open mind, that I will be able to receive clearly what he is saying. And that he can trust me to give dictation of what he is willing to say, and it is like any discourse or communication that goes on in any negotiations.' So I feel here Markos is talking about when countries come together to agree or to disagree, to both move forward in the same way. So when two strangers come together they both put out their hands for a handshake and they measure the worthiness of their, I won't say 'opponent' because they are opposite, and after a skilful start meaningful discourse can be had.

And this is what we are having in countries around the World that are not used to shaking each other's hands. And if there was ever a time for multilateral open-mindedness it is now, when the World is in turmoil both physically and emotionally. When the 'good' and 'bad', and all sides, need to be challenged. And, like two people staring at a candle who see different sides of the flame, they still perceive the heat and the light and the warmth, and that is what Spirit are attempting to do. They are attempting to be the candle in the room in the various discourses around the World. It's almost as if he's showing me like, okay, if you see a circular table on the floor and you have people sitting round it in discussion, politicians or leaders of Government, and then, higher up, there is a veranda that goes round (I don't think veranda is the right word) and Spirit are there. And Spirit are trying to shine the light on the discussions to make it fruitful and to have a more positive impact, and for there to be less aggression and dominance within the discussions. It's almost like, so everybody can see this thin light and they can focus on it and go forward in the discussions, rather than just see the negatives from the other side. Okay Markos, thank you for that, that understanding, and thank you for coming at the request of Bob and myself. Again he bows his head and is receding, having said what he wished to say.

Right, as he recedes, coming forward is **Red Cloud**. I can see a full headgear and his skin is reddish too, whether he's showing it as that's how it was or from the red soil, but he's a beautiful colour. And he comes with a peace-pipe and he puts it down on the table. And he says that although a peace-pipe is worthwhile, it comes after the talking-stick. People cannot hear wisdom if they are constantly talking, and the talking-stick allows hearing to take place, and also for those who don't often get their word heard, it allows them to be heard. And there's a lot of emphasis, he's telling me, on hearing the voices of those that are not normally heard. He's talking about the wisdom of that, and when I ask are we talking 'in the press', are we talking 'children', are we talking 'abroad'? What he's giving me is the principle that you start with your own family and work outwards, so that your community affects another community, and it's about giving those who are unable to express themselves the means to do so. The willingness to listen, and listen without judgement. And I think basically he's saying, if we listened more and talked less, we would all be a lot wiser. He's giving respect to my Guide 'One Feather' and I think that's basically the message that he came to actually share. So before you have the peace-pipe, you need the talking-stick and to listen, and then you can relax in the warmth of love with the peace-pipe. 'What I'm saying is that if you do not listen to all, then it's almost like having a three-legged horse. You don't go far on your journey, but if you listen to everyone and get the full perspective, then you have a happy horse and you can go far.'

He says, 'That will do.' He's also got a big eagle swirling around and I think that's for 'wisdom', so he's a very wise man. And the eagle has very sharp eyes, there's nothing that he does not see. He can see a small worm from a vast distance, not for him but someone else will have that little worm, and then it goes up the food-chain and he will have his food. But he's putting that little worm as something that should be heard, because although it is small it is not insignificant, it has a huge role to play in the earth. It's about looking after the basics, the basis, the earth, it's about looking after the Earth.

Right, **Raja Lampa**. Welcome. I see Ying and Yang, so we're talking about balance. And this comes on from looking after the Earth. There was a transition then from Red Cloud to Raja Lampa, because what he is saying is that 'balance' is essential in the World today, because we have imbalance. In the weather we've got storms, gales, fires, we've got the snow and the ice, and along with that we have temperament the same. We have an imbalance in people's temperament because it is difficult to be peaceful and balanced when the World around you is imbalanced. The way to do that is to sit in meditation in peace and harmony, Ying and Yang. He's saying that all thoughts have a power and although we cannot use our thought-power to alter the Earth's imbalance, by meditating and becoming more balanced ourselves, we will make more balanced decisions. We will live life in a more balanced way and that will assist the Earth, if possible, to regain a balance. The feeling I'm getting with this is that the imbalance has gone over the fifty percent mark and we're heading into bigger and bigger imbalance. And I feel we're down to a slowing of that, rather than a stopping of it. A feeling that we will not stop it, but we can stop civilisation from hurrying up the end of our existence, by living in peace and harmony with the World. And if we were all linked with Spirit, it's almost like a 'blanket' could be put round the Earth to absorb its imbalance and make things right again. But we have a long, long way to go, but hope still reigns.

Pierre. Pierre's showing me food, delicatessen-type food. And he's saying that we should concentrate on quality, not quantity, and where possible with this food he's talking about he's going less processed, from like the plastic, and he's then opening up the cheese in paper, waxed paper, local cheese. So I would suggest here that Pierre also is talking about the global foods. To eat local, only import what we need to, and our health will improve. And again I'm going back to 'Ying and Yang' here with balance. It's almost like years ago there was an imbalance of everything with a physical activity and there wasn't the attention done on an educational side, but now everything's gone the other way and everything is educational and people don't get enough physical activity.

With food, I'm getting wagons of food coming that's bland in colour and bland in taste and lots of it. Then I'm seeing a little market stall all full of locally grown, weirdly shaped fruits with bright oranges, greens, reds, red wine. So Pierre has been giving us the nourishment advice. Now he's looking up to the stars and I can see the sky, jet black with stars up there, beautifully clear. And again we won't have clear skies unless we have clean living. Where we have pollution you cannot see the universe and people are cut off from the Divine.

Now we come to **Pan**. Again I'm seeing like a sieve, you know when they go out looking for gold, gold prospecting, and they put one of those pans into the water and riddle and get the gold out. Okay, this is what I'm getting for Pan. And then he's, we've gone from that taking the gold out, taking the monetary value out, and then seeing someone walking along, sprinkling seeds through it, to make harvest, and to feed the earth. Again that's balance again, from what we take out to what we put in. I'm seeing the moons, the stars, the seasons. So it's to work with the seasons, and then the earth will benefit and we will benefit. I'm seeing like an almanac, I think that's what it is, where they tell you when to plant, what to plant, and I've seen someone just steadily walking at a steady pace. And I think that's what they're doing, they're saying to slow the farming down, go at a steady pace, look after the earth. Let the earth start to repair itself, get back into balance, plant trees. The trees will help us breathe, will help clear the air, it will help stop the rain, the floods.

Then we go to **Philip**. He says he's been listening to all the sound advice that's been given. He's learning it in the 'Halls of Learning', he's learning in Spirit. He's still learning his way, on what he actually wants to do, and when he wants to do it. He seems physically quite strong, he looks I'd say, a young adult in his twenties, and he's breathing strongly. I can see him breathing in deeply, so whether he had a problem where he couldn't breathe, but he's breathing in deeply. [Is he calling you Uncle?] He's asking to be remembered to people that were his family, and for them to know that he's strong. And I think he's been doing a bit of this and a bit of that, because I'm getting him sort of being friends with Dr John and Joshua, going to see what's going on. I don't know whether Philip has any definitive plans yet. He's saying it's an important decision and he's taking his time to see how things develop. Okay, so he's obviously got his eye on a couple of things in Spirit. And I think one of them might be where Dr John was working, about this new discovery, or time-line, that Spirit are working on. I think he's quite interested in that and has got an eye out for that. But he's also looking elsewhere to see which bits, which of the two, makes the most impression on him.

What I'm being told is that each of the people that have given their little message, are in fact **one** message. It is the same message but given by different mouths, in a slightly different way. The balance of the scales, balance is important, Ying and Yang, Spirit and Earth, all is one and one is all, one truth many mouths, many tongues, many colours, many times. When you speak your truth make sure you are holding the talking-stick, and when others speak the truth, listen. 'And we conclude this conversation and we send our love to you our messenger and to our beloved Bob, in love, light and healing. God Bless.'

Okay, I think I'll have to listen to that Bob to see exactly what was said, but I hope they have answered your questions. And I'll leave their love with you and look forward to any feedback that you have. Anne.'

COMMENTS

I do not now intend to analyse the contents which you have just read. I believe the words from each of the Guides speak for themselves. I will however say that I was struck with the tone of their contributions and found them in tune with the 'Teachings' which they had given me in early summer 2017.

Of course the sceptic, or shall we say the critical-thinker, could perhaps conclude, or surmise, that Anne was heavily influenced in her Reading by her knowledge of my manuscript and its contents. While this could be a possibility perhaps, I do know that she has acted as an independent, freelance, 'spiritual medium' for many years. It was through Anne's early Readings that I altogether got to know Dr John and Joshua (though not Philip). Personally I have no doubt that Anne approached her New Year's Reading for me with the same preparation, openness and conscientiousness as she would for anybody. Nonetheless, it is true to say that this was a quite particular task that I had put to her. While I was very interested to see, or hear, what Anne would receive from all the Guides (and thereby also confirm my own genuine contact with them), I especially wondered how Pan and Philip might present themselves? After all these two Beings are not human in the same sense as the other six Guides are. One, I understood, to be the 'Lord of Nature' and the other my 'Guardian Angel'. So how would Anne experience them? You have already read how they came through to her. Pan, visually speaking, in the form of a pan or sieve, and Philip as a strong young man in his twenties.

The symbol of a sieve I had no difficulty with, but Philip seemingly presenting to Anne as a soul or spirit still looking for his task in Spirit, was surprising to me. If Philip is indeed my Guardian Angel then I, or my destiny, **is** his task. That is to say, to help me 'keep on track' with my own chosen way through this life. But, no classically-winged figure of light had appeared!

When I questioned Philip about this human appearance to Anne, he assured me that he was my Angel and that Anne brought him through in a fashion more usual to her main task as a medium. This was not wrong, or incorrect, but it did give a certain 'colouring' shall we say to the way in which Philip could make himself known to her.

Now, interestingly, there was a phrase in Anne's communication with 'Philip' which was not quite clearly audible on the tape. I have included it in square brackets (see above) and I think it said, 'Is he calling you Uncle?' Now this led me to wonder if my niece's son Mathew who died of cancer in 2006, might be coming through then in the Reading? He was aged eleven when he died and in 'earth-time' would now be twenty-three. I therefore put this question to him, to Mathew, and he replied clearly that 'Yes' he had taken the opportunity to come through to me via Anne towards the end of the Reading. On the other hand Philip also said he was coming through as well! So effectively we had a certain mix-up, or admixture, coming through on the same line, as can sometimes happen with a telephone call. Actually it appears that Philip was quite willing to step aside on this occasion so that my niece's son could come through. It is also worth mentioning that when I spoke to Anne, later, about the Reading she said that towards the end she was feeling tired, which probably also had a part to play in the 'crossed line', so to speak. Personally I have no difficulty in accepting that my Angel, Philip, would have graciously stepped aside so that the young man in Spirit could step forward. It was an angelic deed, and also explains why the message, supposedly from Philip, differed in character from that of the other Guides. Moreover it was actually very fitting that Mathew came through, since my previous book, **Spirit Communications**, published in 2007, was dedicated to him. In a sense his presence provides continuity between that book and this one. Mathew had been a chronic asthmatic since early childhood and his earthly birthday was on 12 January, just four days before Anne's Reading for me.

I anticipate that thoughtful readers will have their own questions, and I encourage them to seek their own answers to what has been shared in this book. To learn to 'Trust in Spirit' in no way precludes doing our own active research in freedom and love.

Finally, whereas my first book was very much concerned to describe my personal path of development in learning to know and trust my Guides, and myself, this present book has been focussed on sharing the Teachings given by the Spirit Guides. Teachings which are clearly intended to be helpful to us in our down-to-earth lives, through waking us up to the spiritual dimensions both in ourselves and the wider World.

A third book, still to be written, will aim to bring through knowledge of the Spirit Worlds per se as given by the Guides. It will hopefully answer some of the many questions which people, who are open to the idea of an 'Afterlife', may have. This at least is the plan and, I am already assured, the present eight Guides are happy to cooperate with me in this new research project.

All blessings, Bob

Printed in Great Britain
by Amazon